The
Maeve Binchy
Writers' Club

by

MAEVE BINCHY

with contributions from

IVY BANNISTER, PAULA CAMPBELL,
NORAH CASEY, JIM CULLETON, GERALD DAWE,
SEAMUS HOSEY, MARIAN KEYES, FERDIA MCANNA,
JULIE PARSONS and ALISON WALSH

AN ORION PAPERBACK

First published in 2008 by
Orion Books
an imprint of The Orion Publishing Group Ltd,
Carmelite House, 50 Victoria Embankment,
London EC4Y 0DZ

An Hachette UK company

7 9 10 8 6

Copyright © National College of Ireland 2008

Illustrations by Robyn Neild

The moral right of the National College of Ireland has been asserted.

For further copyright information see pg 168.

A CIP catalogue record for this book is available
from the British Library

ISBN 978 0 7528 8307 6

Designed by Bryony Newhouse

Printed in Great Britain by Clays Ltd, Elcograf S.p.A.

Contents

Preface   vii

Introduction   1

WEEK 1:   Getting Started   5

WEEK 2:   Writers' Groups   9

WEEK 3:   Telling a Story   13

WEEK 4:   Writing Short Stories   17

EIGHT STEPS TO A SHORT STORY Ivy Bannister   21

WEEK 5:   The Writers' Agent   25

WEEK 6:   Sustaining Progress   29

MAINTAINING YOUR MOTIVATION TO WRITE Norah Casey   33

WEEK 7:   Finding Your Voice   39

THE ROAD TO SUCCESS Marian Keyes   43

WEEK 8:   The Writer's Journey   47

WEEK 9:   Visualising Success   51

WEEK 10:   The Role of the Editor   55

THE ROLE OF THE EDITOR Alison Walsh   59

WEEK 11:   The Writer as a Journalist   63

WEEK 12: Writing for Radio   67

   WRITING FOR RADIO Seamus Hosey   70

WEEK 13: Tackling Men's Fiction   75

WEEK 14: The Publisher   79

   THE PUBLISHER Paula Campbell   85

WEEK 15: Writing for Stage   91

   WHAT WORKS ON STAGE Jim Culleton   95

WEEK 16: Murder, Mystery and Suspense   99

   WRITING THRILLERS AND HAVING FUN Julie Parsons   103

WEEK 17: The Importance of Language   107

   LESS IS MORE Gerald Dawe   111

WEEK 18: Writing for Children   115

WEEK 19: Writing Comedy   119

   WRITING COMEDY Ferdia McAnna   123

WEEK 20: Good Luck   129

THE WRITING CLASS *A new short story by Maeve Binchy*   133

Contributors' Biographies   153
Afterword *A Final Word of Thanks from the National
   College of Ireland*   156
Appendices   159

Preface

The Maeve Binchy Writers' Club has been designed to motivate and encourage aspiring writers, as well as to entertain Maeve Binchy fans the world over. The idea first came from a course which ran for twenty weeks at the National College of Ireland, and which aimed to help individuals start and finish a book.

Each week Maeve wrote the students a letter, containing tips and advice on the theme being discussed during the sessions. Then special guest speakers, including some of Ireland's foremost authors, as well as representatives from publishing houses and writers' agents, talked about specific areas of writing. Essentially the programme was about the process of writing a book and the business of being a writer, rather than the craft of writing. Thus it allowed participants to transform an idea into a manuscript ready to be shown to a publisher.

This book comprises the original letters written by Maeve to the members of the Writers' Club, along with contributions from ten of the guest speakers on the programme. It is interspersed with blank pages so that the reader can make their own notes, or even start writing their own short story, poem or novel.

As Maeve says, 'Everyone is capable of telling a story.' This book is the perfect place to start for any budding writer.

Introduction

by Maeve Binchy

This book is for you because you once said or even thought
that you might like to be a writer. This is your special journal.
I've got one too, and we must make them work for us. The
whole point of this book is to remind you that that is what
we do.

We write. We tell stories. We may create poems, do research
into some specialist area, come up with thrillers, turn out a
comedy. But we write. We don't just talk about it.

A little while back we held a course in Dublin where over
two hundred people turned up every week. They heard from
agents, publishers, stage, television and radio producers; they
listened to fellow writers and critics and, in the end, they sat
down and wrote their own books. Most of them finished their
book, and many of them will be published. What really helped
the people attending the course was the discovery that they
were not alone. They were not the *only* people sitting staring
at a blank screen wondering were they mad to try to do this.
They all shared the huge self-doubt which writers know only
too well: who'll want to read *my* take on things? Hasn't it all
been said and done already?

So we decided to make a writers' journal, a book of advice

but with a few blank pages too. Those are your pages. This is what will make the book complete. You could also have your own, separate, notebook, so that you have plenty of space to write longer pieces.

Remember all those ideas or half-ideas that flashed into the mind and just as suddenly flashed out again? Of course you do. Now they can't escape. There's no need to wonder any more if you wrote them down on the back of your cheque book, on the top of an evening newspaper or in the margin of the telephone directory. They will be here in this book.

Suppose you hear a conversation with something marvellous in it, then I advise you to write it down in this journal. A hint is to write nice and small so that you won't use the book up with big, loping writing.

One of the first things I'm going to write is a phrase I overheard as two people passed by my window the other day, talking about a friend of theirs.

'Her feet aren't any use to her ... Not as feet, that is.'

It makes you wonder what on earth they *are* useful as, and there's surely some story it can go into along the way.

If you listen well you will have many more and probably better quotes for yourselves. You will look through them and realise that it would be positively criminal to waste them, and will start writing straight away.

Another thing that you might keep in the journal are details of competitions, prizes or awards. Anything at all that would give us a deadline, a time frame, an urgency to get it finished rather than allowing ourselves to drift on, year after year, saying we'll do it some day. There are some competitions listed at the back of this book, but you can add any you come across, too.

You might also use this book as a place to keep lists of contacts. Suppose someone tells you about a marvellous editor at some publishers; a friendly literary agent; a magazine dying for new writers. Where better to file this information than in your writers' journal?

If you buy this book, or someone gives it to you as a gift, then that means you must be interested in writing. So let's not have that interest remain a pious wish. This is a nice little book. We mustn't waste it. It is not for shopping lists or trying out anagrams for crosswords. The commitment has been made: we now have a writers' journal in our possession.

Yours will be different from mine, but they will all be helpful if they are opened, written in, read and heeded.

There are some pieces of my own, deeply wise advice scattered throughout. You may already know that it's much easier to tell other people what to do than to do it yourself. So I can look back on my days as a schoolteacher and speak with a lofty sense of authority. The most important thing to realise is that *everyone* is capable of telling a story. It doesn't matter where we were born or how we grew up.

I was the first writer in my family; all my relations were grocers or lawyers. They read books by other people, but they thought it was a bit fancy to go and write them. Also

I was from a quiet suburb in Ireland, which is a small country. Who would want to read my stories? But the imagination has no limits. Wherever you are is interesting if you know where to look. Putting your name at the front of this book is your promise that you are going to take this book, and yourself, seriously. Well, seriously enough to do something about this sneaking belief that you can tell a story as well as the next person.

Study all the advice and suggestions certainly, but don't forget your own input. It could even turn out that the blank pages, the ones that you write on, might become the best self-help book ever written. After all, this book will be nothing until you fill it with your thoughts, ideas, hopes and plans.

Good luck to us all.

Maeve

WEEK 1

Getting Started

Writing is a bit like going on a diet; you should either tell everyone or no one. If you tell everyone, then you can never be seen feeding your face in public without appearing weak-willed. So that's a way of reinforcing your decision, and some people find it helpful. It does mean that you're somehow obliged to lose the ten kilos you had promised aloud, or indeed finish the book. Or you could go the other route, and tell nobody – just hug your secret to yourself. Get thin by stealth, write the book, then burst on an unsuspecting world with your new shape or finished manuscript. But whichever way you do it you will need discipline, and some kind of plan.

Time doesn't appear from nowhere. You have to make it, and that means giving up something else. Regularly. Like sleep, for example, or drinking or playing poker, or watching television, or window-shopping or just lounging about with your family. You don't have to give these things up completely but you do have to release five hours a week. So think now where you are going to find them. In my case I gave up a bit of sleep. I had a full-time job in London, a lot of commuting, a heavy social life, a fair bit of travel, so it seemed a good idea to get up at 5 a.m. three times a week. I hated it. Of course I hated it. Who would like sitting at a dining table half crazed

and trying to type, when the rest of the world was sleeping peacefully? Who could enjoy trying to swallow another mug of black coffee in an attempt to open the eyes and focus on what had to be done? In my case what had to be done were ten pages a week, and it took fifty weeks. I could not find those five or six hours at any other time of the day. If I left it to the evening I would be too tired, the weekends held too much temptation, I hadn't the courage to give up the day job, so the dawn seemed the best choice out of a bad bunch.

Now you may be a night owl, or you may have Thursdays off, or quiet weekends, so no doubt you will choose something more suitable for your lifestyle. But you will also have a whole different set of excuses to mine. Like you may have children. So you have to work around them. They must sleep *some* of the time. You may have an unsupportive partner who claims that you are no fun if you are stuck into this book-writing thing. I think you could point out that there are 168 hours in the week, and that you will be great fun for 163 of them. If you want to find those five hours, you will.

A few hints

Keep all your writing things together: computer, laptop, paper, printer, notes, research – whatever. Not everyone is lucky enough to have a study or even a spare room. So what I used to do was keep everything on a trolley under the stairs and drag it out when it was needed. That way I avoided all the time-wasting business of assembling it each early morning.

Mark into your diary each week which hours you will spend on writing and how many pages you expect to get done. If you write that down, you will do pages 34 to 44, then you have no escape and it will stop you sitting there staring at the wall. Accept no interruptions during your five hours: no phone calls, no answering doors, no requests from children to come and play. These are delightful distractions which you will feel that a Good Proper Person should give in to, but you must be ruthless. There are ways round everything, including asking five friends or neighbours or elderly relatives to keep an eye on the children for one hour each.

Finally, listen carefully to all the good advice that follows. And even more important, follow it to the letter!

Good luck!

Maeve

WEEK 2

Writers' Groups

Writing can be very lonely, and you can get great attacks of self-doubt. So in a way it makes sense to bond with a group of like-minded people who have also set out on the same kind of journey. For one thing, it will stop you thinking that you are the only person in the world mad enough to believe that there's a book in you, and for another, it means you will meet sympathetic people instead of dealing with those who think you are crazy and should be learning belly-dancing or car maintenance instead. Let me give you some of my own personal views on the advantages and dangers of a writers' group.

There's a danger that it could become a talking shop. A place where everyone endures everyone else's work as a kind of payment for having them listen to yours – like golfers waiting patiently through the tales of other people's chipping and putting until they can tell their own story.

Then there's the advantage that you can hear the mistakes others make and learn from them. It's much easier to see the flaws in someone else's work than in your own. The man who drones on and on giving endless descriptions of the sunset might bring you back sharpish to your own writing and make you examine it more carefully. Or the woman who

has a cast of thousands of characters confusing everybody ...
This could make you rethink a bit, too.

Another danger I see in writers' groups is that of over-
politeness. I know that I would be guilty of it because if a
fellow member was reading out the greatest load of rubbish
with an eager, delighted face I just could not be sufficiently
cruel as to say how bad it was. And then I'd be afraid that
others were being similarly over-polite to me. Perhaps your
group should have a policy on honesty.

A writers' group would have the great advantage of keeping
you up to scratch like Weight Watchers does, or Alcoholics
Anonymous. If you have to turn up with something written
every Wednesday, then it's easier to keep to your schedule
than if you only had to deal with yourself. It's dead easy to
make a convincing argument to yourself. We have all done it.
'You're tired, Maeve, don't be so doctrinaire, you don't need
to write *every* week,' and so the slippery slope begins. It's
harder to explain to a group that you were tired. They were
all tired, but they did their writing.

Another danger about a writers' group is that it might
make you feel inadequate. Suppose there are one or two

confident writers in the group who are very good; it could send you back into your shell. Or worse, you might want to denigrate your own work and imitate them instead. This would be a pity, but I have heard of cases where it has happened. Anxious people compare themselves unfavourably with leading lights. They feel confirmed in their belief that they are no good and quit before it's really begun. Maybe they were always going to do so, but it's sad when the very vehicle of mutual support and encouragement which was supposed to help them actually just makes them too scared to really give it a go, and is somehow proof that they are right to opt out.

Despite these few dire warnings, I do believe that writers' groups can be a great power for good. I have a friend in England who went to a group, and they all hated each other's novels-in-progress but liked each other. They all gave up on the fiction-writing and wrote a cookery book instead. They got it published, and four more in a series after it, and still meet every week and are firm friends. I suppose, like everything, it's up to you what you bring to and take from a writers' group. I hope that a lot of you may go that route and that you will be able to exchange information and constructive criticism. You probably have much more courage about being honest than cowards like myself. I think my problem was that for years I had a neighbour who used to say proudly, 'I speak as I find.' The thing was that she invariably found something unpleasant to speak of.

May it be very different for all of you!

Maeve

WEEK 3

Telling a Story

They say that when beginning a story you should always try to catch people at some interesting juncture of their lives, like when they have to make a choice or a decision, or when someone has betrayed them, or at the start of love or the end of love. It's better to come across them at some kind of crisis than in the middle of a long, lazy summer where nothing happens.

The notion of change is important in a story. It would be a dull tale indeed if the hero took no notice of the disintegration of his family, if he was the same unaltered dullard after four hundred pages. The reader would feel fairly short-changed.

I can't tell you what story to write. Nobody can do that except you. But I can share with you some of the advice I got along the way from wise editors, men and women whose job it is to know what people like and to keep us writers somehow on the rails.

They told me that we must be *interested* in the hero or heroine – that doesn't mean making the person into a walking saint or goody-goody, but it does mean giving them a strong and memorable personality. There is no point whatsoever in spending pages and pages describing someone who is a dithering, dull kind of person without purpose, views or motivation. Nobody will finish such a story. We have to care enough about the people to follow them through to the last page. When I first heard this I began to panic a bit and asked humbly what kind of people might be interesting enough to hold the reader's attention. I wouldn't be able to create Captain Ahab, the man who pursued Moby Dick, or Rhett Butler who didn't give a damn. But I was told that writing wasn't a matter of painting by numbers. They couldn't just create some formula leaving me to join up the dots. I had to *think*, and work out the kind of people whose lives and adventures I would be interested in myself. This way I might be on the way to make others interested in them too.

In my case I was interested in people who were told that if they were good they would be happy, and were therefore disappointed when it didn't always turn out like that. So I worked out that, in a way, people create their own happiness not just by being good, whatever that is, but by seeking opportunities, taking chances, taking charge of their own destiny. It interested me for a start, and then kept me going. It could work for you, too, if you found a theory around which to base a story, but there's no point in anyone else telling you what to write about. You'll end up writing their ideas, not your own.

Another good piece of advice I got was to think of the story as a journey. Something happens to the main character at the start, and we follow him or her dealing with it, or not dealing with it, or ignoring it, or making it worse. Whatever. Now I don't mean a literal journey, they don't even have to leave home. But they have to progress, be different people for better or worse at the end.

The man who thinks his wife is unfaithful, his son on hard drugs, his colleagues in the office on the take or his own gambling is out of control, has to do *something* to change the situation. You can't leave him static in the same plight at the end of chapter fourteen as he was at the outset. The woman who has had a bad medical diagnosis, a faithless friend, an unjust accusation of shoplifting or proof that her brother is a murderer must have taken steps of some sort over whatever it is. She can't sit there like a dumbo for page after page letting it all wash over her.

They also stress that pace is important when you are telling a story. Again, nobody can hold your hand over this, but I have found that at the beginning it helps to make a kind of chart of the book chapter by chapter, giving myself orders like, 'By the end of chapter two we must know that she cannot afford to pay the rent and will be evicted', and then, 'By the end of chapter three we must know that her rent will be paid for her, but at a price.' If you do this in advance it stops you dawdling about till you're ready and generally dragging the thing out and making it endless. There's no right pace or wrong pace, it's up to you. A gentle lyrical story will call for one kind of speed, a fast-moving action thriller another. But there's no harm being aware of it.

I hope it's all going well for you and that you are getting your ten pages a week done, as I am myself despite a broken arm and a general wish to do anything rather than write.

But I told you it was easy, so I have to believe it too.

Anyway, there's a sort of solidarity in numbers.

Maeve

WEEK 4

Writing Short Stories

This week I had to write a short story for an anthology, and I thought the best help I could be to you is to share all the questions I asked myself and how I attempted to answer them.

Where to set it?
In my case this was easy. It has to be about Dublin, so I placed it in a small house in a Dublin street which used to be working-class but was moving upward in parts. This would mean I could have all sorts of neighbours if I needed them – but I remembered it's only a short story, so no time for a rake of neighbours.

When is it set?
I think this anthology is more for a younger readership, but then again almost everyone is younger than I am, so I decided to make it present-day and see it from the point of view of a restless fourteen-year-old who is dissatisfied with her parents and over-impressed by her stylish aunt who comes to visit.

What are the main dangers in a short story?
For me the biggest danger is overcrowding the story with too many people. No time, I kept telling myself, to bring in her

schoolmates, her teachers. No time for all the neighbours and their problems, no space to talk about her two awful younger brothers. Instead just mention the two insufferable boys as a horrible presence in the background.

Before you begin, what must you do?

You *must* know the end. Otherwise you are lost. I have begun far too many short stories which died the death because I didn't know where they were going. You don't have the luxury in a short story of not knowing how it will turn out and waiting until you see how the characters are getting on. I had to force myself to write down the resolution. What was

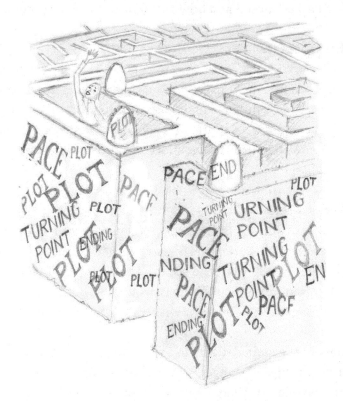

going to happen to the girl's relationship with her aunt? Would the aunt guide her through the drama or be useless? Would the girl know the difference between wise and crazy advice? I was tempted to start writing it and see how it went, but do this and you are sure to end up waffling.

OK, so you know the end, how do you begin?

I think you open with the action, introduce the two main characters. I began with the girl waiting for the aunt's annual visit. I don't do much descriptive stuff at the start. If I were to tell you all about the house and the garden with bicycles in it, and the wallpaper and the shabby stair carpet it might fill in the texture but I'd still be writing it a month later. Get them up and running and start moving them towards the end.

A lot of dialogue or not?

Enough to move the story on. The girl's mother could say something that shows us what a hard life she leads, the girl should say something that lets us know how vulnerable she is, and something else later showing us how she has moved on.

What kind of a time frame?

In this case, for my plot it had to take place over a period of two years. So if I am moving them on at that pace there's no time for long descriptions of what they had for breakfast, nor too much 'he said' and 'she said'. I was tempted to follow the aunt as she went from one cultural event to the next, but if I *did* follow her the plot would never have taken place and the aunt and the reader and I would still be stuck at some exhibition.

How long is a short story?

It's a bit like asking how long is a piece of string. In this case they didn't specify a length (it is actually easier when they do). Anyway, it was about 3,500 words. That's eight pages of my typing. It took one day to plan it out and four days to write, at about four hours each day.

Is it any good?

I have absolutely no idea. I vary in my thinking. Sometimes I look at it and believe that it's tender and sensitive, then I move on and the next day I truly think it's a load of rubbish and that the anthology will return it in disgust.

But I'll tell you what it is … it's finished!

Maeve

■ *Short stories are satisfying, complete pieces of fiction, and many writers use them to practise their art. But where do you start, how do you finish and, most importantly, how do you make it the best it can be? Ivy Bannister's eight-point plan offers some excellent suggestions.*

Eight Steps to a Short Story

Ivy Bannister

1 *Identify your obsessions* What interests you passionately? What is your brain constantly chewing over? Motor-car racing or breeding orchids? Harassment in the workplace? Stroppy teenagers? Your father? Whatever it is, that's your subject matter. It's easier to write about what fascinates you, and your enthusiasm will seduce your reader, too.

2 *Characters* It's tough to do without them. You'll probably have a central character whose perspective shapes the narrative. Scribble down what you know about this character. Don't be shy. Have fun. The more you know, the more your story will flow.

3 *Focus* A story needs a goal, a target, a climax. Or, more formally, a point at which your characters' lives are changed for ever. Get some kind of idea of what this might be –

however hazy – before plunging in. Why do you want to tell this particular story? What is its denouement?

4 *First draft* So you've identified your subject, characters and a target: now it's time to get started. Dump everything you have to tell on to the page as fast as you can, not bothering at this stage with polished sentences or choosing exactly the right word. Aim for your goal. When you get there, congratulate yourself. You now have the bones of your short story. That's the good news. The bad news is that the perspiration lies ahead – but not quite yet.

5 *Research* In flinging out your first draft, you may have realised that there are holes in your narrative, things that you don't know. Now is the time to find out more about your characters and their world. Say, for example, you are writing a story about your mother. Make a list of the things she says, her disagreeable – or agreeable! – habits. Peek into her wardrobe, and take notes. Or perhaps your story involves someone who breeds rabbits. Go to the library and find a children's book, preferably, about the subject (adult books are long and complicated – you want the basics, fast). The internet can be helpful, too. But don't overdo it. The purpose of this research is to enrich your narrative, not to become an expert on the subject.

6 *Producing a polished draft* This is the bit that separates the writers from the scribblers, and it takes a long time. Inch by inch, you develop your messy first draft into a flowing, coherent narrative where every word earns its keep. Good stories are not written: they are rewritten.

7 *Editing* When you think you've done the business, put your story aside for a couple of days. Then come back and tighten it. Cut a lot, because less is more. We all repeat ourselves in casual conversation, but you don't want to do that in a short story, or your readers will abandon you.

8 *Final draft* You're now too close to your work to make the final touches, so go off and literally forget your story. Write another one! See the world! Come back with a cleansed palette, which will enable you to make yet another set of revisions, which will produce the fine-tuned, excellent story that has a chance in a hundred of being published.

Finally, enjoy! If you don't, your reader won't.

WEEK 5

The Writers' Agent

I once heard a writer say that finding an agent was as fraught and complicated as finding a spouse, and there's a lot of truth in that. If it works it's terrific, if it doesn't it's worrying and depressing and there's the feeling that one side might want to get out of it and the other doesn't.

In an agent–author relationship there's plenty of room for a minefield of misunderstanding. The agent thinks the author should be speedy in the writing and the rewriting, yet endlessly patient as regards waiting for responses and results. The author thinks that the agent who is, after all, getting money for old rope, like ten per cent of everything here and fifteen per cent of transatlantic deals, should be back in twenty minutes with news that the Hungarian rights have been sold for a fortune. The agent hopes that the author will understand the frustrations of dealing with busy publishers, writing endless letters, arranging meetings, jogging editors to read the manuscripts they have sent them. The author assumes that the agent knows how vulnerable and foolish we feel as the hours and days crawl by with no word until the eventual humiliating news: 'I'm afraid they've decided to pass on this one.'

So do we need an agent at all? Is it all more trouble and angst than it's worth?

I believe that we *do* need agents. Badly. And here are six reasons why:

1 Publishers listen more to agents than to us. An agent gets a track record of offering readable, saleable stuff, so the publisher will look at it more favourably than at our tremulous, tentative offerings where they can almost smell the quivers of hope and fear in our submission letters.

2 An agent is like a broker who knows the right place to send a manuscript. We could waste months submitting to people who only buy poetry when we are trying to sell science fiction.

3 The publisher is inclined to respond more swiftly to an agent than to us. They don't want to alienate agents; after all, even if they hate our manuscript, the agent could quite possibly be representing someone marvellous next week.

4 We haven't a clue about money, advances, rights, reversions, translations, remainders, reprints. Why should we have? Our job is to write. Agents are more than welcome to their percentage in exchange for taking all that off our shoulders.

5 It's in the agent's interest for us to do well. Any sane agent would prefer to have a percentage of 20,000 euro than 500 euro. An agent will talk us up rather than sell us short.

6 An agent can be our greatest ally. They can tell us when we are waffling, they can head us off at the pass before we go for ever down a wrong track. *They* can say that the lead character has become a pain in the face or that our coincidences are ludicrous. We will take it from them because we travel the same road together, sharing success or failure. Often we can take criticism from an agent more easily than from a loved one.

So how do you find one of these magic agents?

The usual channels are the *Writers' and Artists' Yearbook* (published annually by A&C Black), and *The Writer's Handbook* (published by Macmillan). I hear that agents like a one- or two-page summary, to prove that you have a plot, three chapters to prove that you can write, and the return postage to show that you realise most agents get fifty to a hundred manuscripts a week.

What will make your submission stand out?

If you have had *any* success in any relevant field let the agent know. Perhaps you've had articles or a short story published before, or you actually work in a circus or on a deep-sea trawler where the story is set. Whatever it is, tell the agent. And however gibbering you feel, try to sound confident. No agent wants to take on a bag of nerves; life is hard enough already.

Good luck in your trawl – after all, a lot of it *is* sheer luck, chance or coincidence as well as persistence.

Warmest wishes,

Maeve

WEEK 6

Sustaining Progress

How much easier it is to write a bossy letter urging you to Sustain Progress and to Keep At It than to do these things myself! This morning I should be tackling chapter seven of something, in the sure and certain knowledge that chapter six was endless and droned on and on until it would drive anyone demented. All my confidence and enthusiasm about the story have gone, I would as soon go out and help the people drilling the street outside our hall door than get down to writing. So mercifully today I have an excuse ... I have to write a letter to you.

But – and this is the big but that I want to share with you – I *will* go back to chapter seven this afternoon, because I have this notion of myself that I am reliable and I want to live up to it. I'll finish the damn thing even if it kills me. It's all a matter of discipline, I tell myself firmly, as if this will solve everything. Actually I'm not at all disciplined, and despite my self-delusion I'm not even very reliable. This is just a myth I spread about myself. I heard myself saying yesterday on the phone, 'The one thing I am is reliable,' and I always believe it at the moment I'm saying it. I think it would be desperate if people said you were unreliable, it would be insinuating that you were dishonest. So that's what keeps me going. I promise

to have it delivered by a certain day, and delivered it will be.

It used to be the case that, quite often, the last ten days before delivery involved being up most of the night. But I'm not able to do that any more, so I have to motivate myself to keep at it on a fairly regular basis. In the next section Norah Casey has some good advice for you about motivation, but I do it mainly by a series of threats and rewards. Idiotic as they sound, one of them might work for you.

1   If I get the first four pages of chapter seven done today and the action has moved on rather than stayed static, I will have a huge glass of Chardonnay and read more of Paul Burrell's book about Diana.

2   If I don't get four pages done, I will sit down and make those three telephone calls that I have been putting off for weeks because they will each involve grief and irritation.

3   A few weeks ago I promised that if I got chapter five finished I'd go to see *The Roy Orbison Story* and be in an

audience of mature people who remembered 'Only the Lonely' and 'Pretty Woman' from way back. I finished the chapter and it was just one terrific night out.

4   I said that if I had not managed to update the outline which was by now going very askew, then I wouldn't go out for a Chinese meal with six women friends. I sat at home stabbing at the machine while they apparently had the time of their lives and revealed all kinds of things about themselves, things that sadly I will now never know.

5   There are long-term treats, too. If I finish the whole book a week before the day it's due I will book us a week in Clifden and spend hours rather than just minutes looking at the scenery and the faces of mountain goats and sheep.

6   If it's all a mad rush, as it has often been before, we won't go anywhere. Just torture ourselves with brochures and thoughts of what might have been.

Now all this may seem appallingly self-indulgent and silly to you, but look at it from where I am. I don't need to write for money any more, and money is always a huge help in the motivation business. I don't want any more fame, I'm loud and noticeable enough already. I'm not trying for awards, I never was. I don't *think* that I have a lot of enemies that I want to confound by being successful. So the normal kinds of motivation are unavailable to me. I have to make up my own rules. So do you. And however glum we might all feel we must remember that this is where the losers give up. We will not be among them.

Warm wishes,

Maeve

■ *There's a huge empty piece of paper looking up at you from your desk, or maybe it's a blank computer screen. But you're up against a deadline, or you've stolen an hour and a half to write, and nothing at all is coming. What do you do? Norah Casey shares her secrets on overcoming the problem of an empty brain.*

Maintaining Your Motivation to Write

Norah Casey

The most frightening experience in any writer's life is the dreaded 'writer's block'. The bleakest of spells, however, can be overcome with some tried and trusted techniques.

First, remember that most writers, even the very successful ones, have suffered from the condition. It is important to diagnose the problem honestly. Ask yourself if your inability to write is due to procrastination or a genuine block in your thought processes. All writers go through periods when motivation is in short supply, and what they suffer from is procrastination rather than true writer's block. Recognising what you are up against and dealing with it is the first step towards getting yourself back to the computer screen. Procrastination is a symptom of many conditions. Stress, lack of energy and time are sometimes the underlying reasons. Many writers – particularly those starting out – have full-time jobs or are full-time homemakers. Finding space to write is the biggest challenge. One well-known writer got up at four-thirty every morning to fit in a few hours before the children woke; another used the time after they went to bed. Recognising the limitations of your working day and making a plan to fit in your writing time is imperative.

Maintaining your motivation to write is equally important. Seasoned writers say that difficulties with maintaining enthusiasm can happen at any time, but often the most de-motivating phase, when procrastination can really set in, is when you are working on a rewrite. Again, diagnosing the problem is the key to resolution. Revisiting why you wanted to write in the first place is often a good place to start. The discipline of writing will only return if you capture that enthusiasm and determination which set you on the road to writing that particular story or novel.

For some the motivation is financial – and there is nothing wrong in that. For others, the desire to see their name in print is the primary reason. However, neither of these spurs will sustain you on the long road to publication. More often, successful writers have an urge to communicate a story or an idea. They begin with tremendous self-belief in their ability to put their thoughts across through the medium of the written word. Even the mildest criticism in the early days of writing can be a significant setback – some may even decide to give up. Writers' groups, trusted colleagues and loved ones are invaluable in helping to rebuild your confidence. As you become more expert at writing, your ability to withstand criticism will improve – to the point, perhaps, where you may even welcome tough critics into your life and learn to trust someone who will tell it how it is.

Some writers say that the strongest motivation often

comes from the doubters around them. They remember a tutor, a friend or relation who put them down and belittled their attempts at writing. Proving someone wrong can be a strong determinant to succeeding as a writer – so remember their put-downs and reaffirm your vow to see them eat their words!

Whatever the reason for your procrastination, remember that there are always antidotes. If you are tired, then get some sleep and return when your energy levels are back up – you need to be rested and energised to write well. If you are plagued with self-doubt, read your work over again, call a friend or join a group. Read what other writers have said about their own periods of insecurity – you will find you are in good company. Many writers throw themselves into housework to avoid getting down to work. Learn to ignore the dust and the washing-up and go straight to the computer – and don't surf the net when you get there! Instead of putting the kettle on yet again, make a pact that you will have a cuppa after two hours of writing. If you are bored with writing, or if you find your thoughts straying and can't get yourself back into the plot, take time out and do something completely different. Go for a brisk walk rather than just turning on the radio or TV. Writing, like any job of work, improves with a disciplined regime. Novice writers often find this difficult, especially when there is no one but themselves to enforce deadlines. Be your own boss and implement a punishment and reward system – set yourself deadlines and treat yourself if you achieve them, and find something suitable as punishment if you don't!

The horror of staring at a blank screen with nothing, not a single thought transferring itself from brain to keyboard, is the most frightening experience for any writer. A true writer's block – not just a period of procrastination – can last from hours, to days, to weeks, months and even, some writers say, for years. At the outset, that lonely struggle between you and the screen can be overwhelming. A genuine block is rarely due to short-term problems, but it is worth going through all of the reasons why your thought processes might have come to a full stop to see if there is a straight-forward solution.

The most common reason for writer's block is problems with the storyline. There are no hard and fast rules as to how to overcome this but, without swift attention, an acute attack can turn into a chronic condition. Start by revisiting the storyline. Have you introduced new elements, and are the characters true to your original outline? (It is common to go off track – sometimes it even improves the storyline.) If you have veered from your original plan then you have to decide whether to rewrite the outline, and potentially the plotline of the story, or rewrite chapters. Both are painful decisions to make, but remember that writing is a work in progress, so revisiting your ideas is an essential element of writing successfully. By focusing on the bigger picture (the framework, context, plot and characters) the details often become clearer.

Many great writers emphasise the need to be simple and direct in your storytelling – write as you would talk. One of the really useful ways of getting over writer's block is to do just that – talk about the story and the problem you have come up against. Speak to friends, your writers' group or even to yourself. Don't underestimate the value of 'thinking time' – in the bath, on the bus, while you walk. You will solve the problem more quickly away from the screen. But don't be tempted to stay away too long. If you are really stuck, then write about something else for a while – try not to lose the discipline of writing as you work your way through it.

Whatever you do, don't give up. All writers go through periods of slumped starts, sagging middles and empty endings, so be honest with yourself about why you are avoiding the screen. Don't call it writer's block unless it really is the full-blown variety. Stay focused on the bigger picture and remember why you decided to write in the first place. Make a list of distractions and keep it next to the computer as a constant reminder of what makes you give in. If you're going to be your own boss, remember that successful managers are firm, fair and consistent – so make rules, work schedules and deadlines and stick to them.

Above all else, enjoy it. Despite the hurdles, remember how privileged you are to have that great gift of writing.

WEEK 7

Finding Your Voice

I never knew what they meant by 'finding your voice'. Not for ages. But I think I know now. I believe it means finding a way to write which is comfortable for you. It's finding the method to tell your story that seems natural and unaffected. That way you're not going to get caught out all the time trying to keep up with some kind of style that you thought might be appropriate.

We should think of Shaw's *Pygmalion/My Fair Lady* where the cockney girl can pronounce perfectly 'The Rain in Spain', but comes totally unstuck in a moment of crisis. I know people in Ireland who have changed their accents considerably, and I have an unworthy wish to wake them in the middle of the night with the news that their house is on fire just to see would they cry 'Jaysus' like the rest of us. I think that finding a voice in writing has everything to do with integrity and little to do with stylistic imitation. If we admire someone a lot then it's tempting to think that if we too wrote like that we would be terrific. Not necessarily so – we could end up just looking like poor copies.

I adore William Trevor's writing, I would *love* to be able to create a relationship, a family, a community, a sense of tension like he does. But there's no point in trying to imitate him, I'd fall flat on my face. Instead I read him with awe, and I wonder is there any trick or writing technique that he has which I might somehow 'borrow'. I have been to talks he has given and even asked questions from the audience, and I have learned a lot.

One thing he said was that if you have several characters and set-ups in a story, the trick is to move on fairly quickly from one to the other. If you are starting to get bored by a scene you can be sure that the reader was bored a page ago. Move on, he says, and it's great advice.

He also suggests leaving a short story in a drawer and not looking at it for six months. That, I am afraid, would be a total non-starter for me. The moment I have 'The End' written, the story is in an envelope or on an email to someone. But in a perfect world William Trevor may be right when he says that if you let a story settle for six months you can see all the mistakes as if they were highlighted in yellow day-glo. Yes, but suppose you saw the whole story highlighted? What would you do then?

The point of all this is, what do we get from other writers? My bossy advice is that you don't want to *copy* other writers, what you want is to 'borrow' some of their techniques and present them in your own voice. It's no use asking any writer, 'Where do you get your ideas?' Oddly, it's the question writers are asked most often and it's almost impossible to answer in any way helpfully. You get your ideas by asking yourself what kind of situation would you be happy to sit down and write about every single week for seven or eight months. Usually it's something you feel comfortable with, like something from your own experience or from familiar territory. Or it could be something that fascinates you, for example, if you were interested in military history and were going to write a historical novel set at the Battle of Kinsale.

My most fervent suggestion is don't allow yourself to believe that if a topic worked for one person it will work for you. That way you are denying yourself the real pleasure of writing, which is telling your own story in your own way. There are loads of hints out there, and I have always found writers are willing to share them rather than hug the secrets of success to themselves.

There will always be plenty of readers keen for things to read. Success is not a pie where everyone who gets a slice has somehow diminished what is left for everyone else. That's not really how it works. Success is more like a cairn, a heap of stones where the more each person gets the more it adds to the general body of work out there. Other writers are there to encourage us to be the living proof that those hours of 'keeping at it' can pay off. If we can learn a little hint here and there from every writer we read, and even more especially from every writer we meet, then we will do well.

Maeve

■ *Novels don't happen without effort, and being a novelist requires dedication and tenacity as well as skill. Writers must be prepared to take time discovering their voice, and writing and rewriting until the prose shines. Marian Keyes shares her no-nonsense approach to the hard work that goes into producing a full-length work of fiction.*

The Road to Success

Marian Keyes

People often ask me for advice on writing a book; because I'm a published author they assume I'm in on some big secret. But the good news is that there's no big secret, and the bad news is that there's no big secret. The advice I give is very practical, and it's advice which people rarely want to hear. But I'm not holding out on you, honest to God – this is really how it's done. First, stop talking about it and sit down and start writing it – word by word. No one else can write your book but you. If you don't write it, it won't get written.

Second – and brace yourself for a cliché – writing really is one per cent inspiration and ninety-nine per cent perspiration. Writing is *work*. Perfect characters, plots and sentences don't spring fully formed from the mind of a writer onto their screen. They are only achieved by time, patience, thought and constant rewriting.

Don't be surprised if your first efforts are shockingly bad – indeed, expect to marvel at the gap between what you want to say in your head and how it appears on the page. But persevere; chances are it will improve. Formally set aside time to write – respect your book enough not to try to fit it in, in bitty gaps, around the rest of your life. This is advice that really seems to rankle – perhaps because there's an assumption that writing is somehow 'magical' so that it almost does itself. But it doesn't. So be prepared to get up an hour earlier every morning, or miss out on *Coronation Street* in the evenings or Saturday afternoons around the shops; if you were learning to drive or speak a new language, you'd devote time to it. Better still, try to write at the same time every day – this seems to trigger the subconscious into readiness.

Beware of setting yourself up as the 'new' Monica Ali or the 'new' someone else: it's always cringingly obvious. Instead write in your own unique voice and be proud of it. Be honest and write for yourself, not for some perceived audience; nothing compromises the integrity of a book like the writer tailoring it in advance to please a certain market.

Write what you know – and if you don't know it, be prepared to research it. If you're not sure of your characters' milieu, your book will lack conviction.

Joining a writers' group is often a good idea; you get advice, feedback, support and an incentive to have *something* written to read out every week.

A few final snippets:

Always have a notebook on your person in case inspiration strikes.

It's better if you have a sympathetic protagonist – readers are less likely to stick with a book if they don't like the main character(s).

No killing off your main characters at the end of the book.

And when your book is finally finished – get an agent! Please. This vastly improves your chances of getting a decent deal from a publisher.

Finally – enjoy it! If you enjoy writing your book, the chances are that people will enjoy reading it.

WEEK 8

The Writer's Journey

We get courage from other people's stories. We get consolation from the way they tell about failures, disappointments and crises. It means that we are not alone. We aren't the *only* foolish, overambitious folk who have a drawer full of rejection slips. It's very comforting to know that the Brian Moores, Graham Greenes and John B. Keanes of this world had to cope with exactly the same thing, and aren't we all pleased that *they* didn't give up?

Marian Keyes has given you inspiring advice with her characteristic good humour, so this should keep you going and help you feel you can do it too. But then Marian goes home, and you go home, and there is bound to be that moment when you say, 'It's all right for *her*, she's bright and funny and can write dialogue like a dream. It's different for *me*.' Well, it is, of course, it's different for everyone. But that's the great thing. If it were the same for everyone then we'd all be writing the same book, over and over. But we each have different experiences to draw on, different hopes and dreams, we find humour in different places, and that's why the book has never died out despite all the predictions that it would. The movies would kill it, they said, then videos, then the computer. It hasn't happened.

Is it pretentious to regard your book as some kind of journey? I think not. We are different people when we finish a book. We have had to face ourselves, think about what matters to us and what doesn't. We have to face our own prejudices and attitudes. And maybe admit that we are more shallow or possibly more intense than we had thought when setting out. None of this is any harm.

I discovered when I started to write that I was much more of a moralist than I had believed myself to be. In my stories I always seem to manage it that the good are rewarded and the bad are punished. I didn't know that was the way I felt about things, and I wasn't altogether pleased. It sounded a bit like a pantomime where people cheer the hero and boo the villain. But then I decided that since this was obviously the way I felt I should examine it carefully and see if there was any merit in it. Eventually I worked out that my characters should find their own salvation, that if people in my books created their own happiness then they *deserved* to be rewarded, and if they messed about and dithered then they deserved to fail. I was happy enough with that simple philosophy, and so it will be with you.

A book *is* a journey. Well, it is if you finish it. If you don't then it's no journey at all, just a series of stops and starts and eventual disappointments. I think that this might be the point in the journey when you pause and examine, for five minutes, the actual possibility that you *don't* finish the book. Only five minutes, mind you, not long enough to think about it as a real likelihood but enough to shake yourself up. If you stop now, let's look at what you have wasted. The money you paid over. The time you spent on something you've now abandoned, all those nights when you could have been going to the cinema or for a meal with friends. You've lost the chance of getting to know yourself better. The feeling that you *did* it rather than just talked about it. The chance of saying to people, 'Of course I finished it.' The possibility of getting it published. The possibility that people might love it. The fact that it could have earned you money – had it been finished. You could have impressed and delighted your friends and family. You could have irritated and confounded your enemies. You wouldn't suddenly abandon a long-planned journey to somewhere just on a whim, would you? Of course not.

Your five minutes are over. You're not going to abandon this journey either.

Bon voyage!

Maeve

WEEK 9

Visualising Success

It almost feels like tempting fate to visualise success. It's like saying to the gods that we know we are going to win when we have a sneaking feeling that the gods mightn't like such a cocky attitude and could easily dash us down. Yet I think it's important that we try to do it all the same. It's a powerful lever in keeping us at it, particularly on those days when *anything* seems more attractive than trying to get the ten pages done. So when Reality kicks in asking us who the hell do we think we are, Hemingway? it's wiser not to listen to those voices. Better to choose the over-sunny way and ask yourself, why *not* me?

When I had my first collection of short stories published back in the seventies, I realised that what had kept me going all the dark mornings when I got up at five-thirty to get three hours at the typewriter before going to work, was the thought of the launch party. I could visualise it, and *did* visualise it every time I dragged myself out of bed and forced down hot black coffee to wake me up. I could see the people coming in the door of somewhere glittering. I could hear them murmuring how good I was to have finished the collection and predicting great things for me. Vain, nonsensical, childish – yes, certainly, but it worked. It kept me at it.

Those were often sad, glum times to be an Irish journalist in London, with bombs, sieges and hunger strikes to report. No wonder I kept looking forward to the launch party. When it happened, it wasn't at all what I had expected. For starters, the publisher nearly fainted when I started talking to him about whether we would have sausages or just cheese spread on biscuits. He hadn't intended to have any party at all. My face crumpled in a mighty disappointment. Why had I been getting up so early for months, I wondered? He couldn't help me there. So I decided to spend one-fifth of my advance on a launch party. Two hundred pounds. It bought two hours in a room over a pub in Covent Garden, some red and white wine and crisps. But there were speeches and photographs and lots of pals there and some booksellers, and I generously invited the publisher, who cringed with the shame of it all and, in the end, it was such a good scene that it fired me to sit down and write the next book.

I have a friend, a writer, who says that he visualised moving at ease with famous writers and that that was what kept him going. He could see himself going into restaurants and saying, 'Hi, Kingsley,' or 'How's it going, Melvyn?' And in the end he did get that for himself, to such an extent that he was buzzing round meeting and greeting so many famous names that he almost forgot to write his own books.

I knew a woman who broke up acrimoniously with the man she loved, and his last words to her were along the lines that she would never amount to anything. She dreamed of the day he would see her face all over the bookshops. And that day arrived. It didn't matter to her that much by then, but the visualising had worked. We have all read how Frederick Forsyth was sacked by the BBC and promised as he left Broadcasting House, 'I'll show you.' And he certainly did.

I was at a ceremony last week where a Captain of Industry told the audience that very little in this world was ever achieved by pessimism. He was talking about companies having to *believe* that they were succeeding, visualising a successful outcome, and then they could all work towards that and would be more likely to achieve it. Now, I think he was really talking from the point of view of management rather than the worker bees. Yet as you get older and more mellow you see wisdom in the most unlikely places, and I think he had a point.

Love from,

Maeve

Maeve's Letters

WEEK 10

The Role of the Editor

Everyone has been busy telling you how it's all in your own hands and it's up to you and you alone whether you get a book finished or not. In a way, of course, that's a good thing. It takes away all the props and the excuses that we so easily rely on. If we firmly believe that we are the only ones who can do it, that there's no cavalry out there galloping to help us, then we are more likely to get it done. But if you have been working hard, and the book is on track, then relax a little because today's thought is about a huge source of help: the editor. This is the man or woman at the publishers whose job it is to get the book into shape for you, for them, for everyone. Editors are amazing people. They don't usually write books themselves but they know what's right and wrong with *your* writing. They should be listened to with great attention.

I'll tell you how editors have helped me, and maybe you will see the role they play. The man who edited my first book of short stories, *Central Line*, said that since this book was meant to be set in London's bedsitter-land it was odd that all the characters spoke with Irish accents. I truthfully didn't know what he was talking about, there wasn't a 'begorrah' or a 'Jaysus' to be found anywhere. But he pointed out that Irish people answer a question by half-repeating the question. 'Are you going to take the children to the shops?', 'Yes, I'm going to take them up to the precinct.' The English would answer the question by saying yes or no.

So we went through the whole book, this editor and myself, anglicising any of the characters who needed it, and it was much better in the end, mainly because you knew who was speaking. Later, when I had written my first novel, another editor went through it and said there was hardly a personal description of *any* of the characters! The reader had no idea what they looked like. I fought that for a little while, saying that I never really remembered much in real life what people looked like, were they fat or thin, blond or dark. I only remembered if I liked them or didn't. Politely she told me that I was the one who was out of step here, and could I try to think of them as Missing Persons where we needed a description in order to find them. And I was glad of that help too.

Nobody in the world likes criticism. It's not human to smile in delight when someone tells you that a character you have slaved over turns out to be a pain in the neck. That happened to me when I invented what I thought was a delightful person – Sister Madeleine in *The Glass Lake*. She was meant to be a wise, watchful hermit who knew the town's secrets. The editor said she was sickening because she was always right. I bleated in her defence for a while but the editor begged me to believe that she would drive everyone mad. I muttered unworthy thoughts (only to myself), like if she knew so much about books why didn't she write her own? But fortunately I kept these thoughts to myself, and made the changes. Like I made Sister Madeleine responsible for a poor little blind kitten getting drowned. Is that all right, Editor? Happy now? And of course she was right, and I'm very grateful. And so I learned to listen well to editors along the way.

There are many good reasons why you should learn to respect a good editor. They are like a second line of defence. You know how nervous and unsure we are anyway, well, if the editor thinks it's OK then that's someone on your side from the outset. And not only just someone, it's a professional. An editor would not be paid a salary by publishers if he or she just came up with turkeys and failures time after time. They know what works and what doesn't. Well, mainly they do. Sometimes they get it wrong. And they are just as afraid of having a loser on their hands as you are of being that loser. They are not the enemy. We play on the same team.

Just as it is with agents, it's easy to come across an editor whose manner grates with you. My advice is to get over that feeling fast. You don't have to be the editor's best friend socially, only a professional colleague. Do your rewrites with a good grace or move on to someone else. But don't shoot yourself in the foot over some petty row. Your editor is your

best ally in the publishing house. He or she will fight your corner at meetings and conferences saying you should have a good cover, a decent promotion budget, maybe even a book launch.

Editors are much more likely to be right about things, like our droning on endlessly or being too flippant or shallow or whatever, than our own nearest and dearest. Once you have got as far as having an editor, you're on the home straight. Handle editors courteously and with velvet gloves and listen to every word they say.

Meanwhile, congratulations to you all for sticking at it!

Love from,

Maeve

■ *Like accountancy or shopkeeping or picture-framing,*
publishing is a business. Although it can be a mystery to
aspiring authors, understanding how publishers work is
essential if you want to find the right one for you. Editor
Alison Walsh offers advice on how to be a professional
in a professional's world.

The Role of the Editor

Alison Walsh

Things you need to know about publishing

As an editor, I am always happy to talk to people about getting published, but am slightly puzzled at the sheer fascination the process seems to hold. After all, I trundle through my working days like anyone else, making tea and cursing the photocopier, and consider myself an unlikely keeper of grail-like secrets, which, if revealed, will turn ordinary mortals into bestselling authors.

If only they knew, I bemoan. When I started out as a lowly editorial assistant at HarperCollins Publishers, it was my job to address Barbara Taylor Bradford as 'Ms Bradford' at all times, to remember to send the authors champagne on their publication day and to have chatty conversations with them when they rang looking for my boss, to distract them from complaining about not getting any publicity for their novel. As editor of Tivoli, Gill & Macmillan's popular fiction list, I was required to make more exalted publishing decisions, but am still surprised by the level of public interest in the industry.

Publishing can seem a mysterious business, I am prepared to admit. First, despite all pretensions to bumbling fustiness, it is a *business*, and a tough one at that, with decisions being made about writers' futures with what appears to be cut-throat ruthlessness. Yet it's a deeply personal affair too, founded on good relationships between authors, agents and publishers.

However, as a writer, you are on the outside looking into this curious world, not really finding any way of accessing it. You send your carefully crafted work, over which you have slaved for at least two years, to some 'name' you have selected from the *Writers' and Artists' Yearbook*. You have no idea who this mysterious person is, or what they like in terms of writing. For all you know, they could be a publisher of religious books and you have written a fascinating exposé of Colombian drugs cartels, but in your quest to be published, you reason, you have to try everyone, whoever they are.

Then you wait for at least a month, wondering if the editor's silence is a good sign, perhaps that you are about to be signed up for a six-figure sum and fêted as the new Dan Brown. Just when you pluck up the courage to ring this Yoda of publishing, a fat envelope plops onto your doormat containing your precious work, along with a hastily scribbled note from the guru to the effect that 'their list is full at the moment'. You spend the next week wishing some dreadful accident on the editor before dusting yourself down and deciding to approach the next person on your list.

It all sounds rather depressing, but my aim here is not to have hopeful writers out there throwing their work into a bottom drawer in a rage, but to offer some practical tips to demystify the process. For example, there are certain market factors nowadays that you probably need to be aware of. Sure, over the last few years publishers have focused on concepts like 'marketability' and the dreaded 'brand', and increasingly large amounts of money are spent on fewer writers. It's also true to say that it's harder than ever nowadays not only to get published but to stay published, and you need to work with the publisher to think of angles to get your book noticed, and constantly to have new ideas to keep your writing fresh. But remember, your goal is to get your work into the hands of someone who will love it and want to publish it, so don't let these unavoidable realities knock your confidence!

On a practical level, what do you really need to know about getting published? Do you need an agent? I think you do. He or she will know the market for your work and will have developed good relationships with editors, knowing which ones to approach. Nowadays, when so few publishers read the slush pile (the rather unedifying name for unsolicited submissions), an agent's representation will bring you to the editor's attention.

Of course, you will still need to approach publishers directly to make sure you are covering all the bases. Now, publishers aren't ogres, but they are busy people who are inundated with submissions, so a few small 'don'ts' will save you from annoying them. First, don't second-guess their market knowledge: 'I think my book on child slavery in the Far East in 1783 would make an excellent thriller' kind of thing. It is your job to write the novel, not to tell the publisher how to do his or her job. Don't ring them up the day after you've sent in your work, asking them if they've received it, or rather, why haven't they read it and made you an offer immediately. And don't pester them continually for a reply because you will only hasten the return of your work with that dreaded note. And, if you can possibly help it, don't send publishers partials or rough drafts of your work, in the hope that they will snap it up: you may face the indignity of being rejected for something you haven't finished writing yet.

That's the 'don'ts'. And the 'dos'? Well, the most important thing to remember is that no matter what, you are a writer. You may not have a six-figure contract under your belt or even a three-figure contract, but you sit at your desk every night and imagine distant worlds and fascinating characters, and you commit your ideas to paper. This, above all, makes you a writer.

WEEK 11

The Writer as a Journalist

I was a schoolteacher from the age of twenty-one to twenty-seven. I had written a few travel articles because in those days (1961–7) people didn't go abroad as much as they do now, and it was easier then to sell a story about a summer in Greece, working at a US summer camp, or plucking chickens in an Israeli kibbutz. Then, when I was twenty-eight, I got a job at the *Irish Times*, running the Women's Page, and for five years I wrote and

organised features. Then I went to write features in London for twenty years. It was the most wonderful training and education, and I am very happy to share with you what I learned during that time.

Urgency

When you write for a newspaper, everything is very urgent, it has to be written today and read tomorrow. This is hugely useful to us writers because it doesn't give us time to dither.

And this is a great help. If you *have* to write six hundred words about Ladies' Day at the horse show or the Rose of Tralee festival then you'll do it. Otherwise you'll be sacked. Journalism means that you can never indulge in the luxury of writer's block. The thought of a blank white column appearing in a newspaper is not one that can be considered, so however uninspired we might feel, we *write* the damn thing. Journalists often say to each other, 'Don't get it right, get it written,' and this is not such a bad rule in any kind of writing. You can always go back and change it later if you think it could be improved, but at least it's done.

Observation

If, as a journalist, you were to do a 'colour' piece, it meant you had to become very observant, and this was good training too. You have to compete with television, and if you are describing something like the visit of Bill Clinton or the opening of the Olympics then you know that ninety per cent of your readers have seen it already on the TV. You have to rake the place with gimlet eyes trying to find something that might not be immediately obvious. It's stood me in good stead over the years, I'm always trying to see something a little different in a situation, something that would make it stand out.

Learning what people want

Newspapers are in daily competition with each other. They are desperate to wrench readers away from all the rest, so they are a good place to learn and understand what readers might want. There's a difference, of course, between knowing what they want and being able to deliver it! But I did learn from letters of abuse and letters of praise what pleased people and what annoyed them. They liked to be stretched a bit but not too much. They liked some of their old ideas challenged but not too radically. If we had known the expression then we would have said they didn't like writers to be too much 'in their face'. So I suppose I learned what was to be my kind of writing then, as a journalist. Not too challenging, not hugely ground-breaking but giving them something which was within their own experience, something they could share. Ireland has changed so much since I started that it's a different world now. You will find different things in journalism to help and encourage you, so keep reading the papers and learn from the journalists that you admire. And if you are ever running out of ideas, newspapers are filled with them. You'd be weighed down with ideas after reading a paper thoroughly.

Can you join in?
It's the same old story. You have to banish the fear of rejection in order to try to write things for papers or magazines. There must be some area of expertise that you have – girls' soccer, Esperanto – can you share it with people in a non-hectoring, non-lecturing way? There are training courses in journalism you could enquire about, or you could ask to review books. Of course they might say no, but by now you will have realised that the attractive physical attributes we writers have to develop are a thick skin and a brass neck.

And so, armed with these, let us cheerfully continue our writing journey.

Love from,

Maeve

WEEK 12

Writing for Radio

We all know the story of the boy who said he preferred things on radio to television because the scenery was better, meaning that it makes us use our imagination more.

There are no limits and few horizons on radio. You can set a story in ancient Rome, in pre-famine Ireland or in outer space without having to worry about where you'll get the costumes or who will paint the backdrops.

Seamus Hosey, who you will hear from next, is the real champion of writers for radio in Ireland and about the best friend we could have on the airwaves. And because of his connection with the various competitions that RTE organise, such as the Francis MacManus and the P. J. O'Connor awards, he is a particular friend to new writers as well. These kinds of competitions have been magnificent stepping-stones for many Irish writers, and if you look at a lot of successful authors' CVs you will find that they began by being short-listed for one of these awards.

So, if you want to write for radio, here are some of my own thoughts on how to go about it.

1 *What exists* I think the first thing to do when planning to write for radio is to take a copy of the radio guides and study them carefully. This way you will see the length of the stories they currently broadcast. Remember how we agreed that it would be idiotic to try to submit short stories about knitting to magazines specialising in military hardware? Similarly, there's no point in writing a forty-minute story if the slots are for thirteen-and-a-half minutes.

2 *Don't fear the BBC* You might think humbly as I did when I was setting out that the BBC, which has access to all the famous writers, wouldn't have the time of day for those of us without any track record, as it were. But actually it's not like that at all. The BBC is broken down into regions and, for example, their Northern Ireland drama and literature people are terrific, and quite rightly think it's a huge bonus having all of us south of the border writing our little hearts out. It makes the pool bigger for them to fish in, so don't be a bit fearful to submit things.

3 *Look at changes in emphasis* These days many radio stations are putting a lot of emphasis on items for young people. That was not always the way, and it's opening up plenty of new possibilities. Listen to them, but not to copy them. They don't want copies of what they have already, they want nice fresh new things from our imaginations. And anyway, that's not the way we work. Research, yes, stealing other people's plots, no.

4 *Radio is very intimate* If you were reading your work aloud on the radio your stomach could quite easily churn itself into a spasm. Thousands of people out there, thousands and thousands of them minding their business, driving a car, making the supper, getting over the flu, and there you are suddenly addressing them all. The good news is that it isn't remotely like that. You sit in a claustrophobic studio with padded walls with a producer and you read to him or her. You have no idea of the crowd out there. It's one of the most intimate forms of storytelling. Good producers smile and encourage you and look riveted. They don't yawn in your face and look at their watches. You will be astounded afterwards that anyone outside the studio heard it at all.

5 *Training in taking it all seriously* One of the good things about having to read our own work, or hear an actor read it aloud, is that it makes us less sloppy. You can't get away with half-explained thoughts if it has to be read. You can't have lazy sentences that sort of trickle into the ground. My cousin, the actress Kate Binchy who reads my stories on radio and audio CD, once telephoned me to ask what something meant. I read it over to myself several times and to my horror realised that I hadn't a clue what it meant. It was gibberish. It softened my cough, I tell you.

6 *Ask for more information* Find out about the radio competitions and enter them. Seamus Hosey will start you off but remember, no amount of pious hopes and wishes equals the actual physical act of filling in an entry form and mailing it to the radio station. We are well served by our broadcasting services in this land. It would be a huge waste of such resources if we forgot to avail ourselves of them.

My warmest wishes to you all, and I'm looking forward to turning on a radio and hearing your work before long.

Love from,

Maeve

■ *For many people, listening to a tense drama or an engrossing short story is as enjoyable as reading, and writing for radio presents a unique set of challenges and opportunities for writers. Seamus Hosey elaborates on exploiting the potential of radio, and how to build the relationship between writer and listener.*

Writing for Radio

Seamus Hosey

Radio fixes the person but frees the imagination

I was a Child of the Wireless. It sat on a high shelf in the farmhouse kitchen not far from the picture of the Sacred Heart, and was treated with almost equal reverence and respect. There was really only one station and that was Radio Eireann. My juvenile escapades at moving the dial, sweeping past Hilversum or Stockholm before happening on the exotic BBC Light Programme or pulsating Radio Luxembourg, were looked on somewhat askance by my grandmother and father, especially when I forgot to change back the station to Radio Eireann before going to bed. Next morning I would awake to my father's muttering about 'that bloody fellow messing with the wireless' as he twisted the dial to restore Radio Eireann to its rightful place, giving out the news and the weather forecast at the start of another day.

To me, now, as an adult, radio is still the most intimate of all the modern media. Through the miracle of invisible sound waves transmitted through the air whole worlds of wonder are opened up to the listener. The limits of radio are set only by the limits of the listener's imagination. As a writer for radio you can set your story or play in the Sahara Desert or on a spaceship on its way to Mars or in the inner recesses of the mind of a prisoner on Death Row. Through a combination of human voices, music and sound effects you can transport the listener to experience another world that does not depend on sets or costumes or lighting or visual effects. Radio does indeed, in the poet John Donne's words, make 'one little room an everywhere'.

After twenty years working as a radio producer, mostly in the Arts, Features and Drama Department, I offer the following few observations for anyone who aspires to write for this most challenging and exciting medium.

1 '*First catch your hare*' It might seem like stating the obvious, as in Mrs Beeton's recipe for jugged hare, but before sending your radio play, short story, poem or features script off to any radio station, make sure your effort is targeted at the right place. Listen to the output of the station to know what is currently in demand. Buy and study the *RTE Guide* or the *Radio Times* or your local paper to see the range of programmes in the schedule, and who is producing what. There is no point in sending your 5,000-word rhapsody on your visit to the Grand Canyon to *Sunday Miscellany* which usually broadcasts contributions of under 700 words. Remember, radio is a medium that exists and functions in time, so you must observe the ground rules of that medium if you are to give yourself a fair chance at success.

2 *Fame is the spur* Competitions are often the occasions that give writers for radio their first break into the business. In RTE Radio 1, the Francis MacManus Short Story Competition has, over the last twenty years, been the springboard that has launched the careers of many Irish writers. Even greater than the financial reward is the experience that hundreds of short-story writers have on hearing their work broadcast on air. For many, it is the beginning of taking themselves seriously as writers, giving them the confidence to continue to explore both inner and outer space. Likewise, the P. J. O'Connor Competition for Radio Drama challenges new writers to employ all the resources of that medium to capture and enthral the listener.

3 *This is true but it may never have happened* The Francis MacManus Short Story Competition has attracted an average of eight hundred short stories each year for the past twenty years. Stories have come from all over Ireland and many from Irish people living abroad, and from writers of all ages and backgrounds. As a general rule in radio, but particularly true of the short story, when you sit down to write don't imagine a vast ocean of listeners out there hanging on your every word. Think, rather, that you are writing for one person and that your listeners are multiples of that one person. Remember too that the listener has only one opportunity to take in what he or she hears on the radio. Your story or play can be complex without being confusing. Something that is conveyed by a glance or a look in cinema, television or on the stage has to be put across on radio through words or sounds.

4 *'Whatever I said was never enough and always too much'*
Samuel Beckett Many of the stories and plays that arrive on
the desks of radio producers are no doubt based on the lived
experiences of real people – whether those experiences
be comic or tragic, nostalgic, sad or joyful. The experience at
the heart of your story or play, whether real or imagined,
must be shaped and crafted using the range of skills available
to the writer. It is not enough for the writer to *tell* us that the
experience is real, the writer must *convince* us. Show us –
don't tell us. This means drawing on the full range of shade
and colour in language; images; dramatic turning points;
characterisation and point of view to make the experience
live in the mind and imagination of the listener.

Finally, in the words of the philosopher advising the
aspiring writer for radio: 'There are only two problems
about writing. Getting started and keeping going.' To that
I would add: 'Knowing when to stop.' Or would you rather
die curious?

WEEK 13

Tackling Men's Fiction

This is a whole new world for those of us who are not male. There's some way in, some code, and I certainly don't know it myself. Way back long ago, Jane Austen said that one doesn't write about what gentlemen converse about with each other, since one has no idea what they *do* converse about. Nothing has much changed since Jane's day, except that we know she was right. There have been books written saying men are from Mars, women are from Venus. Questions have been asked seriously about why men never ask for directions and women can't read maps. It is accepted that men have ways of communicating that we don't understand, there is some kind of system out there that they have the antennae for. I've seen it in action but that doesn't mean I could write about it satisfactorily.

Women do like to talk about their feelings and emotions, and to me that seems easy and natural, but I'm nervous of writing about one-to-one intense conversations between men, in case I get them wrong.

Some authors appeal mainly to men: Tom Clancy, Len Deighton, Jack Higgins, Gavin Lyall, Frederick Forsyth, Harlan Coben, Lee Child, Gerald Seymour. This is neither praise nor blame, it's just a fact. I don't think there's a school of writing that's classified as Bloke Lit, not yet. But it may be the next big thing.

These are five points that come to my mind about writing for men, but check them out with the men in your writers' groups. Let this be the time when the women do all the asking and the listening. The only way we have of knowing whether we are getting things right is to go to the source.

1 *Men like information* I gather this from reading all the authors listed above. They have genuinely enquiring minds that delight in things like how to assemble a Kalashnikov rifle, the exact pecking order in the CIA, the way to fix a poker game or how to track some kind of wild animal. Women usually prefer to know why someone succeeds or fails, how to get someone who has stopped loving you to start again, or how to juggle work and home life. Maybe men like their fiction souped up with facts, and regard too much emotion and wondering *why* people said what they did or behaved as

they did dangerously like those tedious, draining discussions at home with their wives.

2 *Men like excitement* If you look at the subject matter of many very popular male novels you'll see that they are often set in times of war, in high-office drama, in espionage, at the Stock Exchange or in a munitions factory. Men don't seem to relish familiar, easily identifiable situations such as the domestic hearth. They like the action moved on fairly sharpish against a more exciting backdrop. They don't buy into long conversations about the family, the love affair, the betrayal or whatever.

3 *Men like heroes and heroines to be lookers* They don't want to hold the action up while a central figure worries about her facial hair, her drooping boobs, or while he broods about his thinning crown or his insecurity with the opposite sex. Men like the cast to come with a full set of parts looking fine and even a bit glossy, admitting to no inadequacies. Remember James Bond when writing for males – they love his immaculate, stylish gear and snobbish social habits.

4 *Men like shorter books* If you don't believe me, go into a bookshop and check. Where are the blockbuster six-hundred-page tomes for lads? Where indeed? Maybe they are busier than we are, or maybe they *think* they are. Maybe they read and have to read more non-fiction. Anyway whatever the reason, if you're writing for fellas write more succinctly.

5 *There are exceptions* Of course there are. Men loved *Bridget Jones's Diary* because they thought it gave them an entrée to the confused mind of a woman. Writers like Nick Hornby,

Paul Durcan, Roddy Doyle, Michael Frayn and the late Brian Moore all wrote about the frailty of men and the sensitivity of relationships. This is not a gender war, a competition of stereotypes. It's not about which side writes better, it's about a genuine attempt to understand.

My warmest wishes to you all.

Maeve

WEEK 14

The Publisher

When we get rejections, and almost everyone does, the tendency is to regard publishers as the enemy. This is counter-productive. The publisher is our great ally, and the bridge between us and the general public who will read our books. If you look at the Acknowledgements pages in a great many books that have been published recently, you will find the name Paula Campbell included. Writers are always thanking her for believing in them and encouraging them. She must get an incredible number of manuscripts on her desk every year, so in the next chapter it will be terrific for you to get to know a real hands-on publisher and to see the kind of stories that people send in – and even more usefully, the kind of stories she's looking for!

There's a slightly sickening expression in the United States which says, 'Strangers are just friends you haven't met yet,' but that's the way I always try to think about publishers. It stops you getting enraged with them, and jealous of those who have succeeded where you have failed. I never found rage and envy good weapons on the admittedly tough road to getting published. I always preferred cock-eyed optimism and insane good humour myself, and since it worked out all right for me in the end, I'm inclined to recommend it as a way to go. But within that hugely positive framework, there are some practicalities which you can all develop and expand on.

1 *Submitting your manuscript*

It is still best to send a preliminary letter, a one-page summary and two to three chapters rather than the whole book; then if they like the look of it, they can ask you to send the whole thing.

You should leave wide margins and type in double spacing. No staples – they hate those and it tears the pages. Some publishers prefer it not to be bound since they want to turn the pages. (Yes, I know these are slightly nit-picking considerations but there's no point in irritating them before they've even read the first line.)

2 *Send the postage*

Again, it looks trivial but put yourself in their place. Suppose they get a hundred manuscripts a week, most of which need to be returned. You can see how this would mount up. And you *are* asking them a favour – to read and judge *your* writing. I have always believed that we writers should just assume that we pay the return postage. It doesn't look over-humble, it looks courteous.

3 *How soon should they reply?*

I've asked around about this, and the average answer is that we should reasonably expect to hear from a publisher within two months. I know it seems like an eternity to us. Sixty whole long days of watching the mail. But publishers have to send it out to their readers and wait for reports, or get it read in-house.

4 *Keep a copy*
Of course nowadays with computers it's fairly hard to lose your entire year's work. In my youth people were always leaving three hundred pages in a taxi or the ladies' loo of somewhere and never finding them again. I really do know someone whose briefcase disappeared with his whole novel in it and we honestly never totally believed him. There was a lingering belief that the poor fellow was lying to us and it had never been finished at all. But wait. A year later it turned up in the locker of a man who had been a year abroad and had packed it into his locker before he left, thinking it was his. And we all spent the rest of our lives being apologetic and feeling guilty.

That couldn't happen now, but what might happen is that we could lose our corrections, rewrites or alterations. So be sure to keep those as well.

5 *Publishers know the market*

We must always respect publishers as businesspeople. They know what sells and what doesn't. It's their business to know. Otherwise they wouldn't have premises and payrolls and backlists and a yearly publishing schedule. Of course they may get it wrong sometimes – everyone does – but we don't want to dwell on that. It's only yet another anxiety to add to our growing collection. Instead, it's better to accept that they put their money where their mouths are. They take a risk on us every time. And because they see so many manuscripts and are in heavy competition with other publishing companies, they are sharper than we are about what will work and what won't. If I write a novel about some topic, like a rags-to-riches story based on a wronged woman who swore revenge on the rich family that scorned her, I might not know that there are already ten or twelve books on this theme out there and the market won't take another. But the publishers will know – that's their business, and we need them desperately.

Love from,

Maeve

■ *It may be a cliché, but there's little doubt that once the hard work of producing your novel is over, there is still a huge job to be done to get it published. And once the contract has been signed, it usually takes a year before your precious manuscript becomes a physical book. Paula Campbell explains the best way to approach an editor – and the process which follows that magical moment when the publisher says 'yes'.*

The Publisher

Paula Campbell

Sample letter

Dear Mr or Mrs Publisher,

I am not sure if fiction is part of your publishing programme, nevertheless I decided to throw a few chapters in the post to you because I am confident that I have a huge bestseller on my hands, something along the lines of Dan Brown meets Maeve Binchy. My family and close friends all agree with me.

I just started writing over the last fortnight and I have found it remarkably easy. I have not enclosed a synopsis or further outline as I am not entirely sure how the story or characters are going to develop, but I feel you will get a good

*idea from the material enclosed and I am confident that
I will be able to finish the novel very quickly. I generally
write during the ad breaks of* **Coronation Street.**

*I thought the handwritten style of the manuscript captured
some of my bubbly personality which would be good for
publicity appearances on the* **Late Late Show.** *Please ignore
the teeth marks on the corners – had a bit of a tug-of-war
with my dog, who is a little possessive of my work but is
my number one fan. I did not enclose a SAE because I know
that you* **won't** *be sending this back to me! I am happy to
allow you exclusivity for forty-eight hours, otherwise you will
have missed a huge opportunity and I will be targeting
other publishers.*

Regards

The Next Big Thing

The Role of the Publisher

Obviously, this is not the best way to approach a publishing
house (your potential business partner) with a manuscript.
As Publisher at Poolbeg I can receive up to two thousand
manuscripts a year and only publish fifty – so that is a lot of
rejections! While the gift of writing is something to treasure,
you must approach it in a serious way. The publisher's
decision to buy someone's book, assuming the material is
appropriate to their programme, is based on a combination of
many elements including a strong story, good writing and
well-presented material. So do your homework. Find out the
guidelines for submitting manuscripts for each appropriate

publisher and follow them. Send in the best work you can – and then be patient. It is not a good idea to threaten the publisher who is, after all, your first point of contact! You just never know who could be on the way to making your dream come true.

If you do get *the* call (which is one of the nice jobs of being a publisher, I might add) and the publishers want to take on your work, the next stage is the signing of the contract. This may vary from publisher to publisher but in general it will give you a lot of important information regarding finances, rights and publishing timescales. Now the process really begins, and you will soon see that publishers work very far in advance putting together plans as to when and how to publish the book.

About twelve months before publication date the editorial process will start. Editor and author work together on getting the manuscript ready for typesetting, proofing and ultimately to print – seeing the book on the shelf for the first time is a moment to savour!

During that time your book will also be the topic of many publishing meetings with the Production, Sales and Marketing departments, where we discuss:

The best publication date
Taking into account seasonal factors, competition and key bookshop activity, the publication date can be up to eighteen months after the contract is signed.

The format of the book
That is, do we publish in paperback or hardback? Take a look in a bookshop and see the different shapes and sizes of the books; they will all have been discussed and planned at length.

The cover

It is said, 'Never judge a book by its cover,' but that is exactly how many consumers make their choice, especially if it is a first-time author. The cover must tell the reader something about the story, indicate the target audience and, ultimately, jump off the shelves and say *buy me* – a tall order sometimes! The area of cover design is a fascinating and ever-changing one.

The sales and marketing campaigns

These are a vital part of the book's success, and the sky's the limit regarding creative, fun and innovative ideas. We can loosely split this area into two: the sell-in and the sell-out.

The sell-in – getting the book into the bookshops

Booksellers buy new titles about six months in advance. They make their decision based on the cover and what the publisher plans in terms of marketing, advertising and publicity, so most of the time they won't have read the book!

The sales reps are armed with the cover and campaign details and maybe the odd treat or incentive that lends itself to the book. For example, when Poolbeg published *Watermelon*, Marian Keyes' debut novel, a special consignment of gift-wrapped watermelons was delivered to each bookshop – which certainly made a lasting impression. Chocolates and champagne are also popular for some reason!

The sell-out

This is what needs to be done to get the finished books from the shops out to the consumer in terms of bookshop promotions, posters, dumpbins, author events, advertising and, of course, publicity.

A special note about publicity: no matter how good a book is, despite the publisher's best efforts, they cannot guarantee that a book will be featured on the *Late Late Show* or reviewed in the *Irish Times*. The area of commercial fiction in particular is crowded and competitive with an estimated 50,000 books published annually, so the competition for coverage is fierce and the media are always on the lookout for that exclusive angle. Sadly, writing a book is just not enough.

I hope that gives you some brief insight into the publishing process and the role of the publisher. It can be an exhilarating but also an anxious time for an author. Above all, the publisher is also there as friend and confidante.

I wish you the very best of luck. Don't give up, dreams do come true, and remember, without you writers we publishers wouldn't be here.

WEEK 15

Writing for Stage

After twenty-something years of writing stories in book form I *sort* of know that the main thing is to keep the story going, move the plot on, don't go down alleyways and don't introduce a cast of thousands. That's storytelling. But I can't begin to know what will work in a theatre, so now you have a chance to learn at first hand.

Jim Culleton knows what works on stage – he has this extraordinary instinct about what will make people laugh or cry in a theatre. I have no idea how he can look at lines written on a page and see which will work in a dark theatre and which won't. Jim is very approachable, and has always been a great encourager to new writers as well as working well with so-called established writers. Whenever he has taken my short stories and adapted them for the stage I thought they were hilarious, and laughed loudly and immoderately until the audience thought I was insane and very vain. But I was laughing not at my own words (which often looked very flat on the page) but at the way they were presented. So how do you go about writing for the stage?

1 *What do I write a play about?* I know Jim Culleton believes that the best plays are on topics that we feel passionate about. People will write with conviction and ultimately much more success if it's on a subject dear to their hearts. There's no point in wondering what kind of themes might be more successful than others and saying, 'Aha, that's what I'll write about.' It just doesn't work. Remember all those plays in the last century which began with a maidservant dusting a telephone, and had people bouncing in through French windows asking who's for tennis? That all came about because a few successful comedies were set at posh house parties and then everyone thought they could do it.

2 *Do I need to know a play-writing technique?* I think not. But I believe that if you go to a lot of theatre yourself, and read plays, it will somehow sink in. You will learn, as I have half learned, that people don't necessarily declaim, they don't make and finish a speech and then stand back to let another person make a similar speech. Rather they interrupt each other, leave sentences unfinished. You have no time in a play to write interior monologue, which is what I am heavily into. You know the kind of thing:

> *She looked at him, worried. Did he really love her, or was this life they had a total compromise? She would never really know, since he was good at hiding his feelings. Was it better not to challenge him, leave things as they are? Or was this the worst way to go?*

I'm slightly sending myself up here but you know what I mean. In a play you can't give all this background information, you have to get it over by giving the angst-ridden woman some short line which will convey all of the above.

3 *Do you need a large number of stage directions?* Apparently not. That's the director's or producer's job. And sometimes it's the actor's job. They don't want us to write down every move for them. If we get the dialogue right it should all be there on the page.

4 *Are there huge limitations on the time and place in which we set a play?* No, I believe it's meant to be much more liberating than any other kind of writing. In a theatre you can change the whole timescale and have someone's childhood or old age shown just by a change in lighting; or you can have different events taking place in different settings. Again the trick is to go to lots of plays and watch for the possibilities.

5 *Are we mad to think we might be playwrights?* Just as the publishers are not sitting there laughing at our pathetic attempts to write but are actually dying to find something they can publish and make money out of, so it is with theatre folk. They are aching for us to write something that will make them hugely successful and the talk of the town. So all we have to do is to keep at it until we get it right.

Great good wishes and huge success.

Love from,

Maeve

■ *The most successful playwrights are often those who began their writing career drawing from their own lives. They also understand the vital interaction between a live performance and the audience. Jim Culleton examines how to give a play focus, and the unique collaboration between playwright, director and actors.*

What Works On Stage

Jim Culleton

When I was asked to give advice to the Maeve Binchy Writers' Club about what works on stage I remember thinking, 'Well, if I knew the answer to that, every single play I direct would be a huge success.' There are no rules for what will or won't work, but there are a few qualities I certainly look for in a play.

I have adapted Maeve's stories for the stage a few times, and it is always a very enjoyable process as they capture so much of what works well on stage. They have very clearly defined characters, great dialogue and – most importantly – Maeve has something heartfelt, that she believes in passionately, to say in each one. I think playwrights should have a strong vision of what they want to say and then the language and structure should express it in an engaging, exciting way. A director or dramaturge can help with the structure and character development, but the playwright should have the initial passion for communicating a unique view of the world.

The well-known advice that encourages 'writing about what you know' has a lot of truth to it. Certainly, writing about what you know gives a personal and unique insight into human behaviour and relationships and can give a strong sense of truthfulness to the writing. Some of the most successful first plays by new and emerging playwrights that I have directed have often explored situations with which the playwrights were familiar, mixed with their imaginative and creative insight too.

When writing a play, I think it is best not to think of the play as words on a page, but rather of theatre and its possibilities. Plays can be set anywhere – there are no boundaries. Playwrights should feel they can use the possibilities of the medium and visualise actors, set, lights and sound as they are writing. As Maeve says, nothing beats going to the theatre and seeing both what inspires you and what you would do differently as you develop your own theatrical voice.

In terms of how to structure a play, there are fascinating decisions for the playwright to make about the order of scenes and how information is revealed. Some interesting examples of this are the use of the flashback in plays like *Dancing at Lughnasa* by Brian Friel, *The Nun's Wood* by Pat Kinevane and *Red Roses and Petrol* by Joe O'Connor; the reversed chronology of scenes in *Betrayal* by Harold Pinter, a pub full of characters played by two actors in *Two* by Jim Cartwright; the way time and chronology are subverted in *Top Girls* by Caryl Churchill; the way information is revealed through interconnecting monologues in *The Pride of Parnell Street* by Sebastian Barry.

Once the playwright has something passionate to say, and works out how to say it, the next stage – hopefully – is producing the play. Theatre is a live art form and a collaborative one. So it is not as solitary for the playwright as writing in other media can be. Moreover in theatre, directors, designers and actors can help bring a new perspective to the play through their input. In working with playwrights on new plays, I find the most exciting writers are those who strike a balance between being clear and focused about their vision and yet open-minded about how the play evolves and grows as it moves towards being performed for an audience.

Often, on playwriting courses, new writers are encouraged to write a very short play (under ten minutes) that establishes a premise, explores the issue and reaches a conclusion, as Samuel Beckett does in many of his short plays. Perhaps that is a good challenge for any new playwright wondering how to begin!

WEEK 16

Murder, Mystery and Suspense

How I would love to be able to write a thriller, a story that would raise the hairs on the back of people's necks. But I'm bad at suspense. It's a personality thing, a bit like talking too much, wanting to tell everything a bit overeagerly – I'd give away the plot too soon.

I love reading thrillers. I *love* them, and usually read two or three a week. Recently I read John Grisham's *The Last Juror*, *Paranoia* by Joseph Finder and a wonderful old-fashioned green paperback called *Tragedy at Law* by Cyril Hare. I have even gone so far as to write down *Hints on Writing a Thriller* which I have in a notebook. Some of them have been there for twenty years, so I didn't exactly get on with it. In a fit of generosity I have decided to give you all my hints.

How do you create suspense?
Ed McBain has written dozens of 87th Precinct and Matthew Hope novels. I interviewed him once and asked him if there was a rule. He said he had a trick, which was that you gave the reader more information than you gave the cops. Then the reader felt terrific at guessing what was happening before the detective worked it out. He advised against making the police into total fools, however. Evelyn Anthony, who

I also interviewed, says that she does suspense by preventing one set of people from knowing what's happening, so they are heading blithely into the jaws of some kind of danger that we readers know about, but the characters don't.

How do you do a surprise ending?
Agatha Christie (who I did not interview, sadly) once wrote that she began each thriller with the chapter on the suspects' alibis, then she arranged that one of the alibis could be broken and that would be the murderer. She worked out personality and motives later.

False alarms
When you are reading a good thriller you can approach heart failure over some perfectly simple false alarms. A creaking door could be a cat coming in, not an axe murderer; a flapping window could be a trapped crow, not a serial killer making an entrance. And then, just as we are calm again and breathing relatively easily, they pounce on us. Maybe that's something to set up.

Attention to detail

A lot of thriller writers like a fair amount of gory detail, and you need to get that right. Patricia Cornwell and Kathy Reichs have audiences of millions for their pathology laboratory books, but you can be sure that every last detail is correct. Similarly, Len Deighton, Jack Higgins and Freddie Forsyth will have the assassins' weaponry accurate – not a ball bearing out of place. If you choose a specialist area, like John le Carré chose the world of spies, you'd want to be sure to get it right. There are too many old pros out there reading books and just dying to write to the papers or the publishers to say you have it all wrong.

Bring in your own area of expertise

You don't have to throw out your own style just because you're writing a thriller. If you have a witty style, you could write a humorous thriller – or a woman's thriller or a travel thriller for that matter. There are endless permutations.

Those are my hints, but next you have something much better with advice from Julie Parsons. I used to know Julie way back when she was a nice quiet girl, a producer in RTE, and there was no way of knowing she was destined to frighten us all out of our wits with her writing. What terrifies me so much about her books is that they are all set in so-called normal and familiar places, places like Blackrock and Dun Laoghaire. On the surface everything seems normal, that looks like an ordinary family, that looks like a reasonable couple. And then we discover that they are very far from the norm indeed. So how does she do it? Does she have a master plan and tell herself exactly when she's going to pull the rug from under our feet?

Finally, remember that publishers and booksellers *love* the thriller as an art form. So good luck – you could well be the new Conan Doyle!

Love from,

Maeve

■ *Thriller writers understand the bigger questions in life –*
including love, death, greed and anger. They also know
how to encapsulate these things into gripping plots and
page-turning narrative. Julie Parsons examines the crucial
role of the imagination in thriller writing, and how to turn
your ideas into plots.

Writing Thrillers and Having Fun

Julie Parsons

When I talk to people about writing, they always ask why I write the kind of books I write, and where I get my ideas from. Neither question is easy to answer. I suppose one of the reasons for writing a particular kind of book is that you enjoy reading them. I have always loved thrillers – especially those that are called 'psychological thrillers', the ones that are more concerned with motives and relationships, rather than the actual crime itself. My favourite authors are Patricia Highsmith, Ruth Rendell and P. D. James, all of whom write the kind of books that I like both to read and to write. In fact, P. D. James puts it in an interesting way:

E. M. Forster has written: 'The king died and then the queen
died is a story. The king died and the queen died of grief
is a plot. The queen died and no one knew why until they

discovered that it was of grief, is a mystery, a form capable of high development.' To that I would add, the queen died and everyone thought it was of grief until they discovered the puncture wound in her throat. That is a murder mystery, and it too is capable of high development.

The most important thing to remember about writing any-thing is to use your imagination. No matter how much research you do, your imagination is what counts. John Mortimer, who wrote the famous Rumpole series, actually advises that you write the book and then do the research. Plots come from hard work. They won't develop by them-selves. They need to be thought about, struggled over, worked on. I often use the 'what if' method – I constantly ask myself, what if, what if, what if.

I also think that genre fiction, such as crime and mystery, is just as important and interesting as writing that is categorised as literary fiction. Thrillers deal with the really big subjects: death, violence, cruelty, good and evil. They are often all about important moral and ethical dilemmas. They invariably raise the question of nature versus nurture, heredity versus environment, and whether people are intrin-sically good or bad.

Again, P. D. James expresses this very well. She says that all the motives for murder come under the letter L: love, lust, lucre and loathing. She also says that the most dangerous emotion of all is not hatred, but love.

If you want to write a novel – in any genre – one thing is very important. You must be filled with desire. Writing novels is very hard work. It requires a huge amount of dedication. In order to carry the project through from start to finish you really have to *want* to do it. But it's important not to get too discouraged or put off by what seems to be the magnitude of the task ahead. The American writer E. L. Doctorow puts it very well. He says that writing a novel is like driving across country at night. All you see ahead is what is lit up by your headlights. But if you just keep following your lights you will eventually reach your destination.

Keep at it. Your hard work will be rewarded.

WEEK 17

The Importance of Language

I was at a funeral recently and heard a man speaking from the heart about his friend who had died. They had shared a love of the sea, and his words had a lot of maritime metaphors about tempests and storms and coming safely to harbour and back to shore. It was exceptionally moving, and thinking about it afterwards I wondered why it had affected us all so much. I decided that, as well as its obvious sincerity, it was the careful choice of language and the way he had used words. He made sure that not only will we remember the content, the fact that we all missed his friend who was a good man, but

we will also remember the way it was said, the setting that the speech had been given as well as the speech itself.

In my own writing I have always been careless of how I choose words, believing that the important thing is to go on quickly while the idea is there, to tell the story, to get on with what happens, not to delay by rolling round a phrase until it pleases me, not inserting a nice melodious sentence just for the sake of it. I have often been afraid to pause and choose words that will appeal.

This is a definite if not deeply offensive flaw in my character which I hope I will not pass on to you. But if too much of it has stuck to you then now is the time to shake it off. Gerald Dawe, a poet and scholar who really does love language, will help you release the vocabulary that you have inside you. Because he has read so much, and deals with words every day of his life, he will be able to encourage you and set your feet firmly and unselfconsciously on the path to expressing yourself more fully. But first, here are a few thoughts of my own.

1 I wonder, do the Irish, or people living in Ireland, have a bigger word pool? Or is that madness? My own view is that it's a definite advantage to come from a culture that once spoke a language with no words for Yes and No. You had to get round Yes and No if you were speaking Irish, like saying it is or it isn't, or I will or I won't. It meant you had to say more and make longer sentences. Other people who came to Ireland both before and after J. M. Synge are taken with the slightly convoluted way we speak. They think that we can be fairly lyrical without even trying. So I regard that as a bit of a bonus.

2 Another advantage of being Irish is that we missed the Victorian bit that the British went through, of not talking until you had something to say, or children being seen and not heard, or speaking only when you were spoken to. All of these notions are utterly alien to the Irish psyche. But is it good or bad for us? Perhaps those folk who take more time to think things through come up with better words. Perhaps we are, for all our much-admired fluency, just motormouths.

3 In one of Kurt Vonnegut's marvellous books – I think it's *The Sirens of Titan* – there is a tribe whose people only use words that they like the sound of. This was a great idea for a while since they sounded so melodious, but the tribe died out because they had no way of communicating with each other. Words had no meaning, only good sounds. That always stuck with me as a possible danger.

Sometimes when you read very pretentious book reviews and articles there are words in them that *nobody* could understand. One I keep seeing and having to look up is 'palimpsest'. It means a manuscript in which old writing has been rubbed out to make room for new, or a monumental brass turned over for a new inscription. I know, I know, you're going to tell me that you use the word palimpsest every hour of your life. But to my mind it's showing off, and obscures language rather than enriches it.

Love from,

Maeve

■ A writer's job is essentially the skilled manipulation of words. The use of language can establish character, describe an atmosphere, drive a narrative forward or impose a point of view. Gerald Dawe discusses the use of language, and how the way in which you say something is as important as what you say.

Less is More

Gerald Dawe

For any prospective writer, the principal, most basic of issues is the use of language. I want to show you in as uncomplicated a way as possible that no matter what your objective is in writing – whether it's to please yourself, to communicate something to others, to make money or to 'be known' – the only really important issue is how you use language and how alert you are to different kinds of language.

First, let me issue a warning: I want you to think about how vulnerable language is to manipulation, distortion and misuse. Have a look at George Orwell's great essay, 'Politics and the English Language'. Then let me give you just one example of the weight of meaning transmitted by language. A few years ago the *Irish Times* published a letter in the aftermath of the IRA murder of Detective Garda Jerry McCabe, and it sums up perfectly the way words can be loaded with extra meaning. It's very short, so I reproduce it here in full:

19 February 2004

Madam,

The Sinn Féin TD Arthur Morgan writes compassionately of the 'prisoners convicted of involvement in the tragic events that led to the death' of Garda McCabe. Is this clumsy phrase a new euphemism for 'convicted killers'? Yours, etc.,

Tony Allwright, Killiney, Co. Dublin

All writers, even unpublished, first-time writers, have to bear in mind how language can be twisted and turned into propaganda. By not saying how we see and hear things, of what we know to be the case, we sidestep reality, and that is not good for a writer; any writer.

Good writers are always good readers and good listeners.

No matter how naturally gifted you may be with, say, description, or plot, or characterisation, the more you read, the better your chances of learning more about what you want to say. All writing is about learning – learning to do what you do *better*, trying out different forms, concentrating on the work in hand, rather than the 'impact' or reception it may or may not have. This is equally true of fiction, non-fiction and, of course, of poetry. Maybe in bringing a poet's experience to the subject I can underscore the need for all aspiring writers to focus on *how* they were saying *what* they were writing.

Have a look at a couple of John McGahern's short stories, 'Faith, Hope and Charity' and 'High Ground'. They are marvellous examples of a sparse, lyrical and astute use of language. From the descriptive detail to the dramatic setting, recorded speech and the unsaid, enigmatic suggestiveness of the writing, I want you to see how 'less is more'.

If you want another example, in Hugo Hamilton's powerful, emotionally intense yet controlled memoir *The Speckled People* there is a marvellous scene towards the end, set in Dun Laoghaire on a fogbound pier, when the viewpoint of the young man, filtered through the imagination of the mature writer, creates a physical mood. And that mood conveys the story and propels the narrative to its resolution.

Writing fiction is an extraordinary freedom; to sit down and create characters, scenes, moods, feelings, ideas, beliefs, with comic, tragi-comic, light-hearted, serious, entertaining intention must be one of the hallmarks of our human individuality. The next step – to publish – is another day's work. I can't explore in any detail that crucial stage, as others are doing that, except to say that publication should be the final priority, not the first.

But to call upon the great cliché: at the end of the day, using language is very much like learning to listen, *really* listen, to other people, including, bizarrely, oneself. The last writer I want to recommend to you is the English poet, W. H. Auden. This is a marvellous passage:

> *A genuine writer forgets a work as soon as he has completed it and starts to think of the next one; if he thinks about his past work at all, he is more likely to remember its faults rather than its virtues ... He needs approval of his work by others in order to be reassured that the vision of life he believes he has had is a true vision and not a self-delusion, but he can only be reassured by those whose judgment he respects.*
>
> The Dyer's Hand, 1963; 1987

And so say all of us.

113

WEEK 18

Writing for Children

There was once a theory that writing for children was somehow easier than writing for grown-ups. Not any more there isn't. And there was once a belief that children's fiction was a quiet little backwater. J. K. Rowling has put an end to that theory. Today's children are well catered for with thousands of books appearing every year and huge sections of bookshops devoted entirely to them. Children's authors have rightly got their place in the sun at last, and people have recognised that writing for future grown-ups is very important.

Even though I don't write specifically for children, I do know a fair bit about it because I'm married to a children's writer, Gordon Snell. The world of children's writing has a very different set of highs and lows to the so-called adult one. If you are giving a reading for children and they are bored, they don't just yawn or drop off to sleep as adults do, they get up and go away. Adults *always* ask you where you get your ideas, and are deeply disappointed with the reply, which is, 'from all around you, from looking at things and people and listening to them'. Children ask you more interesting things like how much did you get paid and how many pencils did you use?

Children often read a favourite book over and over, getting something new from it each time. That's a fearsome responsibility to have when you're writing a book for a young audience – the knowledge that they may well know your book by heart in a few weeks. You can't be lazy and let things go if someone's going to give it that much attention! Here are a few questions to think about if you want to write for children.

1 Do children need simpler language, or do they come to terms with words that they don't quite understand? Sometimes when we were young we'd come across an unfamiliar word and because of the sense of the story we'd get to know what the word means. I remember years back there were often words used by A. A. Milne and Lewis Carroll that I didn't know, but I sort of *got* to know them. When writing for children, should we stretch them or adapt our vocabulary to suit theirs? I genuinely don't know.

2 Do children want us to use their particular slang? Would that make them identify better with the story? And if so, what kind of slang or colloquial speech should we use? It does change a lot, doesn't it? And they might be saying 'deadly' one year and 'gross' the next but it could have changed utterly the following year. Is it wiser not to explore the slang minefield at all?

3 Is there still a huge difference between what boys and what girls read? Nowadays with more co-education is there a blurring of the lines?

4 How do you avoid patronising children? Roald Dahl certainly knew how, as does Eoin Colfer and the whole galaxy of successful and popular children's writers these days. I think it's hard if you're a teacher to begin with. You start trying to improve them, trying sneakily to teach them something. They can smell a teacher a mile off. They'd have me sussed in two minutes.

5 These days children all love electronic games, and texting each other and watching television programmes where you can phone in, so how can we hope to engage them in something that's not interactive? Or is it the same as in the adult world – like the Death of the Book that everyone feared so much and which just hasn't happened?

As with all writing, the best advice I can give is to read other authors you admire in the same field, and see how they deal with these questions.

Only one more letter from me – my genuine congratulations that you've stuck with it. You *deserve* to be successful because you have taken on board the notion that it's all about keeping your bottom on that chair and refusing to give up.

Love from,

Maeve

WEEK 19

Writing Comedy

Oh to be able to make people laugh at will! Wouldn't it be wonderful? To see a lot of glum faces and turn them magically into happy ones! No wonder great comedians and gag writers are paid a fortune. No wonder Hollywood gets so excited about a zany or wacky comedy with someone like Steve Martin, Woody Allen, Eddie Murphy or Leslie Neilsen. Is it any surprise that publishers yearn to find the book they can call Comic Novel of the Year? But how to do it? That is really the question.

There really *is* such a thing as the art of writing comedy, and Ferdia McAnna is well placed to tell you how to do it, he who could make us laugh hard at what everyone had thought might be tragic material. Ferdia, who takes work seriously but has never taken himself seriously, is a very good role model for anyone who wants to write funny and doesn't quite know how. I think the worst job in the world, worse even than being a dentist or a miner, must be to be a stand-up comic. Imagine standing up and telling what you thought were jokes and people not laughing! An audience of them not laughing. It makes me feel weak and as if I were going to vomit at the very thought. Suppose you think something is funny and nobody else does? Does that make you mad, or make them mad?

I remember telling a story once that I thought was hilarious. I still feel the sweat on the back of my neck at the memory of it. Everyone stared at me politely waiting for the punchline – after I had delivered it, long, long after. I wanted the world to end. I remember thinking, it has to end *some* time, why not now? But it didn't and I had to get on with living and I swore I would never try anything funny again. But we swear things and we forget them. And so when I recovered I tried again, and sometimes I got a laugh and it was so heady and so wonderful that it was all worth it!

But writing comedy is different. We aren't there to see and hear whether anyone is laughing or not, and so it's equally difficult for a publisher to know whether or not something is going to entertain the readers. All right, we would all love to have people splitting their sides at what we write, and if there was any easy way then surely someone would have discovered it. Why was *Dad's Army* such a scream for so many people? And *Fawlty Towers* and *Absolutely Fabulous* and *Father Ted* and *Cheers*? Was it the characters themselves? Or the plot situations? If we knew, we could do it too. But we don't know, so we have to try to find out – without copying other writers – what on earth makes people laugh.

1 Sometimes I think they'll laugh if we make ourselves look foolish, vulnerable and a bit silly. One of my most successful articles in the *Irish Times* was about not knowing whether to make the bed if you stayed in a hotel. It was utterly true. I had never stayed in a hotel until I was twenty-two. I sort of straightened the bed and folded back the covers, nothing that would destroy me as a hotel visitor. To my amazement, half the country seemed to have had the same dilemma, and they were delighted with me and told me I was a wonderfully humorous person, whereas in fact I had been telling the unvarnished truth in the hope that it would make people less self-conscious rather than amuse them.

2   Sometimes people laugh if you can create a truly funny character, like a clown figure, somebody you are meant to laugh at. But this is very hard to do. If you go over the top and make that person into a caricature then it's not really funny any more, it's only a stereotype. You keep thinking that if that person was played by Bette Midler or Barbra Streisand she would be a scream. But she's not being played by them, she's just by herself on the pages of your manuscript. You have to make her so appealing that readers like her as she is without any first-rate comediennes delivering her lines. I've tried saying lines aloud to see if they're funny. Half the time it doesn't work – maybe more than half the time – but it's worth giving it a go.

3   As a journalist, over the years I have interviewed lots of funny people for the newspaper. I have met S. J. Perelman who wrote the Marx Brothers scripts, George Burns, Bob Hope, Dave Allen, Victoria Wood, Maureen Potter. They all said, every single one of them, that they had no idea whether something was funny or not until they tried it out.

All writing takes courage. Maybe comic writing just takes more courage than the other sort.

Love from,

Maeve

■ *Comedy has been used for centuries as a way to entertain, to satirise and as a defence against tragedy. One of the greatest skills a writer can have is an ability to recognise comedy when they see it. Ferdia McAnna explains how to look for comedy in everyday life, and where to go for inspiration.*

Writing Comedy

Ferdia McAnna

In Ireland, it often seems that anyone is capable of coming up with a humorous remark that can provoke a laugh but haunt the victim for life. Some years ago, a disgruntled politician described the then Minister for Finance's contribution to the economic debate as having subtracted from the sum total of human knowledge.

I imagine that few Irish writers nowadays would describe themselves as 'Comic Writers'. The label Comic (or Comedy) Writer is as limiting and slightly ludicrous as wearing a clown's red nose, and perhaps not something you'd like stamped on your passport. The area of Irish comic writing is neglected and often ignored. There has been very little attention paid to it in recent years, despite the worldwide success of Roddy Doyle and Eoin Colfer, just two Irish writers whose work strongly features humour.

Comedy is a difficult thing to define. What makes one

person laugh may leave another feeling indifferent. The only sure thing about comedy is that it is personal. Nobody can tell you what to laugh at or explain why something is funny. Attempts to persuade a person of the hilarity of a prose passage can often end in humiliation and resentment, or, at least, disgruntlement. About the best thing you can do with comedy is recognise it when you see it. Yet comedy, humour and wit are so deeply ingrained in the Irish character that we in Ireland often take them for granted. It runs through Irish writing, even in work of an essentially tragic nature such as Patrick McCabe's dark masterpiece *The Butcher Boy* or John Banville's acclaimed *The Book of Evidence*. Humour, along with literature and music and, more recently, the international soccer team and Riverdance, is one of our ways of communicating with the world, and an essential ingredient in our daily lives. You can find it in the wit and thrust of everyday conversation; the delight in wordplay and mischief; the rapture in telling and embellishing a good story and the sheer, sometimes malicious glee in the Irish national pastime of 'slagging', a basic philosophy of humorously criticising or insulting someone for the sheer sport of it – or until the victim loses his or her temper.

Dethroning the pompous is as ingrained in Irish writing as the delight in satire, parody and the grotesque. This spirit was traced in an unbroken line back to ninth-century bardic literature by Vivien Mercier in *The Irish Comic Tradition*, the key (and only) work on the subject. Mercier concludes that the Irish comic tradition, far from being a peripheral activity, can in fact lay claim to being the central tradition in Irish literature. In other words, Irish literature would be nowhere without the craic.

It may be true that Ireland has never had to suffer the

horrors of a world war, unlike Germany, England, Russia, France and other European countries. Yet the catalogue of disasters to have beset a small country is still fairly comprehensive – eight hundred years of occupation, various disastrous uprisings and insurrections and political and social disunity, the twin holocausts of famine and mass emigration, years of violence in the North, not to mention the stifling power of the Catholic Church. Against this backdrop, it is tempting to view the Irish love of comedy as a defence against hard times and oppression. The early Irish wakes, for example, were often ribald affairs. Traditionally held in the presence of the corpse, the wakes featured singing, dancing, the telling of obscene tales, even the occasional orgy as well as an amusement described as 'performing tricks on the corpse'. In *Finnegan's Wake*, Joyce's word for funeral was 'funferall'. Curiously, while we celebrate great writers such as Joyce, Beckett, Heaney, Shaw and O'Casey for their humanism, their modernism and their innovative use of language, we are often slow to pay tribute to their comic gifts and to acknowledge the comic tradition that has influenced and indeed inspired much of their great work. Perhaps we prefer to regard comedy as a type of natural human fallout, a spontaneous emission that enables us to get through life, rather than an art form that requires toil and intellectual rigour.

Nevertheless, comedy writing is a tough business. If a writer's particular brand of comedy fails to impress a reviewer, then that writer's work stands a fair chance of being dismissed as shallow, unconvincing and laden with stereotypes or, at best, tolerated as harmless gas. In today's supercritical climate, the writer of comic literature can often feel vulnerable. As Spike Milligan put it, 'Naked, I had a body that invited burial.' Many Irish writers use comedy as an essential ingredient in their work – from the greats such as Beckett, Molly Keane, Maeve Binchy, Roddy Doyle, Frank McCourt and Joseph O'Connor to emerging writers such as Paul Howard, Emer McCourt, Paul Murray and Claudia Carroll, as well as the not so well-known, left-field, neglected or maverick talents like poet and prose stylist Pat Ingoldsby.

Why is comic writing so undervalued? You could blame the ancient Greeks, who invented theatrical comedy in 486 BC as mere light relief to their productions of tragedy (the word comedy is derived from the Greek word komos, 'to revel'). Aristotle wrote that the difference between comedy and tragedy was that 'comedy aims at representing men as worse than they are nowadays, tragedy as better'. He concluded that the origins and early history of comedy were obscure because it was given scant respect. In other words, tragedy traditionally portrays man as noble and heroic, whereas comedy usually reveals him as an ass. As William Hazlitt wrote, 'For every joke, there is a sufferer.' In Irish life one of the great contradictions (and great jokes) is that the very language the vast majority of us use to express ourselves belongs to another country. Gaelic words and rhythms have influenced the English we speak in Ireland and have flavoured our writing, but a great deal of Irish comic writing is virtually indistinguishable from its English counterpart. Irish humour, while difficult to define, usually shows two distinct emphases – one on fantasy and the other on the grotesque and the macabre.

To the Victorian poet and critic Matthew Arnold, the Celts and particularly the Irish were 'sentimental', 'overly imaginative', 'exotic' and 'always ready to act against the despotism of fact'. That tradition of acting against the 'despotism of fact' is in excellent shape today. Indeed, perhaps the only true difficulty with Irish comic writing – as well as its greatest irony – is that nobody takes it very seriously. Nobody, that is, except for the writers and the readers. And that's the way it should be.

Some tips for the budding comic writer

1 Write about what you know – and that includes your family (especially your family).

2 Ignore the facts.

3 Use your imagination, and don't let anyone or anything put you off.

4 Break your routine. Whenever you feel yourself settling into a groove, go for a walk or phone someone you hate or attend the wedding of a complete stranger.

5 Enjoy what you write. Because if you do, there's a really good chance that the reader will, too.

6 Always remember George Bernard Shaw's famous remark about comedy: 'Always tell the truth – it's the funniest joke of all.'

Enjoy!

WEEK 20

Good Luck

Well now, does it seem like a lifetime since we began? Or did it go by far too quickly, before you got to grips with it all properly? In any event – congratulations! Well done for sticking with it. The very fact that you stayed means that you have a real commitment to being a writer. It's more than just a pious wish now. You've invested the time and effort and therefore proved that you do take it seriously.

I hope that in the marvellous selection of contributors you found not only inspiration but consolation. It's surely helpful to know that it's not easy for *anyone*, and that you aren't the only one who has been insulted by rejection. It's part of the training process. I am sure you learned from everyone, whichever side of the editorial process they are on, that they know rejection is worse than failing any exam because it's so personal. And yet it's our testing ground. There is no structure where we pass or fail, we just have to keep hoping and keep sending stuff out.

What will separate the winners from the losers is that ability to pick ourselves up and refuse to take the rejection personally. The courage to say, well, that person may or may not be right but I'm not going to stop. The very fact that someone has dared to send you back the beloved manuscript you slaved over and told you, though not in so many words, that it was useless is obviously a blow, but if this book has taught you that it happens to everyone, then it has probably given you hope rather than despair. I wish that hope to stay with you always. It is what will eventually draw out of you the book, the stories, the writing, that is in there waiting to be released.

None of us ever stops learning. For my last novel I got seven pages of closely typed corrections or rewrites from the publisher. Now this is after sixteen books, so it goes on and on! I read them humbly and changed everything that I was asked to. It doesn't get any easier to do rewrites, but then we don't necessarily get any better. I *still* forget to give personal descriptions of people; I know what they look like so I assume everyone else does. I *still* forget that you have to get people from one place to another, even a sentence saying that they went to the harbour, or they went back to her flat. I always think the reader knows automatically where the scene is taking place.

I promised to write twelve short stories this year. I have six of them written, two of them published and one commissioned for the radio. And each week I wrote a letter to you, which I actually enjoyed very much. It made me think seriously about the job I do and how it's done. For the last twenty-five years I suppose I've been a bit on autopilot and I just get on with it. It was a challenge to try to think for you and for myself what technique is involved writing a short story; what your relationship with an agent should be like; how to set up a thriller. I had to think hard about what works on stage or on radio.

The idea of this book is to take the terror out of writing, to empower ourselves with the belief that we are as good as anyone else with as much to say as the next person. The only thing that stands in our way is *not* saying it. I hope you think it was all worth it and that you will never be among those who say that you could have written if only you had had the chance. The chance was offered to you, and you took it up bravely and enthusiastically. From now on, when we see each other's books in the shops we will take a vow to move them to the front of the store.

Solidarity is everything.

Love and well done,

Maeve

THE
WRITING
CLASS

by *Maeve Binchy*

The woman on the radio made it all sound so easy. It was a matter of having a beginning, a middle and an end, having some sort of a plot and listening carefully to the way people talked. All over the country they listened to her, and people's hearts soared.

A class that would teach you to be a writer, it was *exactly* what so many people were looking for. Women in their kitchens preparing supper paused to write down the telephone number, students meant to be doing last-minute revision scribbled it down on their ring binders. Men stuck in jobs that they hated wrote it down and dreamed of the day they would have a book launch and invite only those they had liked in the office. Motorists pulled into the side of the road to write down the number.

It seemed like money for old rope.

Nancy was none of the above. Nancy was packing her things to leave Ed's apartment where she had lived for three years. It was over, Ed had told her, and there was no point in trying to pretend otherwise. It was time for everyone to move on. And they should do it sooner rather than later.

Ed wasn't moving on. He was moving a new person in. He asked Nancy to be gone by Saturday. He would leave her a couple of days to sort it out on her own. New beginnings for everyone, he had said cheerfully. He would change the locks on the door Saturday morning. Better that way.

Nancy was going through the bookshelves taking her books, which was most of them. She looked through the CDs:

most were his, but she would leave them all. It looked like a big, generous gesture on her part. In fact she would never want to hear the music they had played together. Never again.

She thought about the bedspread. It had been very expensive but it had been a birthday present from her to Ed. She wouldn't take that. The picture they had bought in a gallery in Cornwall. They had each paid half. She wouldn't want it on a wall in her new life, it would remind her too much of those magical days in little Cornish harbours when the world was full of hope and sunshine and promise. The saucepans? His, really. Towels? She didn't want them. Just her clothes, and the books and a few ornaments. Not much to show for three years. Not much to take to her new quarters.

She had rented a big bedsitter with a tiny kitchen and an even smaller bathroom attached. She was telling nobody how it had ended, how cold and detached Ed had been, how he would dare to change the locks as if she would ever come back here again. She could not humiliate herself by admitting that she had lived three years with such a man.

None of her friends liked him; nobody at work knew about him. Nancy worked in a florist's shop. The woman who ran it was very reserved, and she discouraged any chat about people's private lives. In many ways it had been a relief. No need to explain that Ed had gone away without her yet again, or that there was no sign of a ring or a commitment of any kind.

Nancy looked at the radio. His, if you were being honest. But then he had taken her old radio and traded it in for a better one. So now she had no radio. She wondered would she take it. Maybe it would be petty. Better leave with an aura of generosity. Even though Ed had shown very little sign of it. It had good tone, that radio. Nancy switched it on for a last time and heard the woman talking about the writing class.

That's what she would do. She would write a bestseller. Ed would see her books in the windows of the bookstores, he would see big feature articles about her in newspapers and magazines, he would turn on the television and see her on chat shows. He would learn of the huge advances she would get for each novel and what a fortune she was earning.

Ed loved money. He would be very regretful that he had sent her out of his life. And changed the locks. Very. Let him have the radio. She had written down the number she needed on the back of a picture of her that he still had in the bedroom. She had left the frame so that he could put the next girl in it. Nancy wondered, would she last three years?

Then she called a taxi, locked the door for the last time and put the soon-to-be-useless keys back through the letterbox.

Jane ran a bed-and-breakfast business. It was tiring and it was hard work, but it was a living and she actually enjoyed meeting the people who came in and out. At the moment she was full, all four rooms occupied. Two with eager Scandinavians, couples who had, it seemed, already walked the length and breadth of the city and were setting out to walk still further. One bedroom was taken by a wordless man who came up from the country for four nights every week, and the secret police of no country would prise from him what his business was.

The fourth room was for Lilly and her six-month-old baby Sophie. Jane hadn't really wanted to take Welfare people and have the house full of screaming children. But Lilly was so young and the baby so quiet that she had no excuse. When the other guests had finished breakfast, Lilly helped with the washing-up and making the beds. In return, Jane gave her full use of washing-machine, drier and the kitchen. It worked well as long as nobody suspected. Jane got paid by the authorities, poor Lilly and Sophie, the baby, had something near a home, and nobody lost out.

Jane had never trained for any career. She had always looked after her own mother, who had been poorly for as long as anyone remembered. And then when Jane was forty, Mother died and there she was with no real way of earning a living. Her brothers had shrugged, Jane had lived in Mother's house for all those years when they had to go out and buy places of their own. It had all turned out very well when you came to think of it. Yes, very well indeed. An empty house and no qualifications.

So she started the bed and breakfast. She went to computer classes and learned how to get visitors on the internet. She considered borrowing from the bank and putting on three more rooms at the back, but eight people was manageable for breakfast. And she had grown fond of Lilly and Sophie. Building work would be too disruptive for a baby.

Jane didn't have extravagant tastes, she didn't really need more money. All she needed was the sharpness of mind to make sure that her clients weren't the sort who would empty the house of her simple belongings. And really, the B & B business wasn't that bad. You were finished by eleven in the morning, with the house clean and the shopping done for tomorrow's breakfast.

Jane took in ironing in the afternoons. Her own little bed-sitting room had two clothes rails in it, and she had got to enjoy the smell of freshly ironed shirts. Sometimes she offered a guest the luxury of ironing something for them, and they nearly fainted with delight. So she was at her ironing board when she heard the item on the radio. It doesn't matter what kind of a life you lead, the woman appeared to be saying. If you could tell it like a story, it would work.

Jane paused, iron in hand. *That's* what she would do this autumn. Join a writing class.

Vincent and his son Gerry listened to the item in the car as they drove home from the graveyard. It was the first anniversary of Sheila's death. They had gone to put flowers on her grave. They had hoped it might make them feel better, but it had made them feel worse.

'You were a great wife,' Vincent had said to the small Celtic cross over the grave.

'You were a great mam,' Gerry mumbled, as if they were lines from a school play. He had been in the school dramatic society before, but somehow since Mam's death he hadn't the heart for it.

He had nothing to say to his father and his father had no words for him. They were driving back to the house that seemed to have no soul in it these days.

Vincent turned on the car radio. 'We might as well be listening as not,' he said.

'Sure, Da.'

It was some writer telling them about a class which taught you how to write a book. They both listened because it was easier than trying to talk when there was nothing to say. Eventually the woman was replaced by someone else who was talking about keeping llamas in your garden. Apparently you could have four llamas per acre. Vincent and Gerry managed a watery smile over that as an idea.

Then Vincent said, 'You know, your mother always said I should write a book about my adventures on the road.'

'Did she now, Da?' Gerry wondered what possible adventures his quiet father could have had as a travelling salesman driving a van all over the country.

'She said it was a story of the old times, before marketing came in and changed everything,' he said.

'Well, maybe you should join up at the class then.' Gerry wanted to get his father out of the house for some sort of thing. This might be as good as any.

'I'd be afraid to go on my own, I don't have any confidence going to social things any more. Would you come with me, son? Maybe they could get a book out of you too?'

His father was pleading. He had never seen this before. Gerry heard himself saying that he'd love to go.

'A pity we didn't write down the phone number,' said Vincent, who seemed very pleased by this decision.

'I wrote it down, I've got it here,' Gerry said, and the car was a lighter place once the plan had been agreed.

In the radio studio they were packing up.

'The llama piece was nice,' the series producer said approvingly.

'I thought your woman who was doing the writing class was good,' said the presenter, Clare.

'Oh, God, no, another one of these "everyone's got a book in them" gurus.' The series producer had seen it all, done it all and was impressed by nothing.

'Maybe we all have,' the presenter said defensively.

'Oh, please Lord, then let's hope that everyone keeps the book well buried inside them, rather than releasing it.'

The series producer was busy putting on lip gloss. She was going to have cocktails with some very smart people who were thinking of putting money into an independent production company. This just might be the big crossroads in her life. She had little time to make idle chat with Clare, a girl who was fast on her way to nowhere. She hadn't noticed that Clare had written down the phone number of the writing class and had every intention of joining.

On the first night of the writing class they heard that they didn't have to pay their fees until the first lecture was over. This would give them a chance to know whether or not the course was right for them. There were questions they would want to ask. Nobody should join unless absolutely certain that this was the right course. At the end, almost every-one signed up.

They were put into groups of five. The hope was that they would help each other and encourage each other if anyone was failing to write the ten pages a week that they would be expected to produce.

The first week would be an easy assignment: they were to go around bookshops and libraries and see what kind of book they might possibly write. They were to list the publishers they might approach; then they were to write a letter to an imaginary friend telling the story.

They were urged to introduce themselves to their group. Clare the radio presenter met Nancy a florist, Jane who ran a small B&B, Vincent and his son Gerry. Vincent was a salesman, his son about to go to university. They all had coffee and biscuits and reassured each other that they weren't completely mad to be doing this.

Next week they would all meet again and read each other the letter to the imaginary friend; then they would have a lecture from a publisher listing the most common mistakes people make when submitting work.

'I suppose we should think of it like Weight Watchers or Alcoholics Anonymous,' said Jane.

Vincent nodded thoughtfully. 'Great people, those AA folk,' he said. 'My wife was a member and they would go out in the middle of the night to help each other.'

Gerry's head shot up in alarm. His father rarely mentioned his dead wife, and to Gerry's certain knowledge had never told anyone of her alcoholism.

Nancy rescued the moment. 'Right – if we are going to be open all hours then we should give everyone our mobile phone numbers,' she said in a businesslike way.

They went home into the dark.

Nancy went past Ed's flat to see was the light on in the bedroom. If it was dark, that meant they were in bed making love. If the light was on, then it meant that they were so confident with each other they were making love with the lights on.

Jane went back to the house where she had lived so long with her mother, a house with a B&B sign swinging in the night air now. She hoped that Lilly was up so they could have tea and maybe toast and honey. But the house was silent. The

Scandinavians were absolutely exhausted from pacing the city. The wordless man from the country was asleep dreaming of the Lord knew what. From Lilly's room, Jane heard muffled tears. It was one of those nights when Lilly's broken heart was hurting worse than usual and she was wondering why the boy had run away from her and baby Sophie.

Clare the radio presenter went home to her parents' house where she lived fairly peaceably with her mother. Except for the times when her mother was urging her to get married. Tonight turned out to be one of those nights.

'I suppose it was all women at the class,' she said glumly.

'There were some men there, but you're right, it was mainly female.'

'Not much hope of meeting anyone there, then.'

'No, Mother, but then that's not what I went there for, I'm going to learn how to write a book.'

'Huh,' said Clare's mother.

'Leave the girl alone,' said Clare's father. 'She has plenty of time to meet someone.'

'And when I do want to meet someone I'll go online or answer a lonely hearts advert, so don't panic, Mum.' Clare wished they had asked her about the evening. But she was a grown-up woman of twenty-four now, not a child any more. It was silly wishing for impossible things.

Vincent and Gerry went into their house where so many promises had been made and broken about alcohol. Where there had always been secrecy, and new hopes that had not materialised. Vincent took out a couple of cans of beer. Gerry's eyes opened wide. Because of Mam there had never been any form of alcohol in this house.

'We have to move on, Gerry lad,' his father said. 'If we're going to write ten pages a week then by God we need something to get us started.'

The next Tuesday they all turned up in good time and settled around the little table in the hall. They all had their ten pages ready.

Nancy read her story-letter. It was about a good woman who was involved with a monstrously selfish man. She then made a great deal of money and he was sorry that he had let her go and begged her to come back. But she wouldn't. Then he fell on hard times so she relented, returned good for evil and went back to him.

The other four looked at her blankly.

'It's not very likely, is it?' Jane asked. 'I mean, I know nothing really about anything except serving eight cooked breakfasts a morning, but why would this woman go back to him if he was so awful? Wouldn't she be far better off on her own?'

Clare said she thought if we were meant to think the heroine was barking mad and heading for the funny farm we should be told more. It couldn't be the twenty-first century. Women didn't do that kind of martyr thing any more.

Vincent said that it hadn't been made clear in the outline whether the woman and the monstrous man had a really wonderful thing going between them once and it had drifted away because of some problem.

Gerry said he thought it would be a better story if the woman were to kill the monstrous man. Maybe by electro-

144

cuting him in the bath. It could be written in such a way that we would be a bit sorry for the woman, and hope she got only a short time in the mental home.

Nancy was very disappointed with this reaction, but she nailed a smile on her face. And they went on to hear Clare's story.

Clare had written about a woman who had a job on the reception desk of a big insurance company. A horrible woman senior executive in the company was constantly putting her down, so life wasn't very cheerful. At home things weren't much better. She had parents who were very much on her case for still being single. They made her feel a failure. What she really wanted was a chance to live in a big house with lots of other young people, like in the television sitcoms. And then one day there was an advertisement for flatmates and she found exactly what she was looking for.

Jane always tried to say something nice, but she wondered if this was a touch unrealistic. If this receptionist was so good, why didn't she just get on with things at work? And if she hated being at home, why didn't she just move out? She must have some friends to move in with rather than finding the advertisement ...

Nancy didn't want Clare to think that she was reacting badly just because her own story had been shot down in flames. But she did say gently that the heroine lacked any sense of purpose, and if we were meant to identify with her she'd have to do something more than complain.

Vincent said that there was no mention at all of how the heroine related to her parents. Did she like them or just resent them? After all, they were probably just trying in their hopeless, ham-fisted way to do the best for her. We couldn't like her unless that side had been explored.

Gerry said that he thought the heroine should kill the senior executive by stretching some thread across the stairs which would cause the senior executive to fall and break her neck. The heroine should have nail scissors ready and remove the thread while pretending to be concerned. Then the senior executive's job would be offered to the heroine and she would have plenty of money, get her own flat and tell her parents to stop worrying about her.

Jane looked at Vincent, hoping that he would go next, but he gallantly waved a hand at her and encouraged her on. So Jane swallowed and told her story. It was about a woman who had spent her whole life since she was seventeen looking after her invalid mother. She had got no thanks, no recognition and no recompense for it. Her brothers had been free as birds to find love and careers for themselves. They were married with children now, but they did not make her part of their families. The woman had met a lonely, neglected mother on social welfare, a girl hardly more than a child herself but who had a little baby, and eventually she decided to take them into her house and make a family for them all ... Jane stopped and looked around the little group. It was the usual silence.

'Well, it's a nice idea,' said Clare, 'but it doesn't go anywhere – remember they said there should be some turning point somewhere, where people do one thing or the other and that's what makes the story?'

'And what's the point of her being bitter about the awful brothers *now*?' Nancy asked. 'If she's going to be bitter it should be when the old woman is alive, and she should make them each take their fair share. No use when it's all over. It's a bit feeble of her, wouldn't you think?'

Vincent said it was a hard premise to expect us to think that a woman who looked after a frail parent was somehow a loser. Most people did what they had to and got on with it. The reader wouldn't have any sympathy for the heroine – unless of course she made a really good home for the unmarried mother, but how could she do that if she had no job?

Gerry said that it should turn out that one of the brothers had murdered the mother, and the heroine should discover this and blackmail the brother into giving her a house.

Vincent cleared his throat and said that his story was about an alcoholic man who made everyone's life very anxious because he had long periods off the drink, and just when they were all relaxed he would suddenly go back on the drink again. And when he was sober he was the most wonderful sensitive man in the world, and no one ever discovered why he went back on it.

They waited, but that was it.

Nancy said that, to be very honest, they should remember what had been said at the opening lecture. It wasn't up to us writers just to create mysteries: we had to solve them, too.

Jane said that in the end everyone gave up on mystery people: she had a regular guest in her house who was so secretive that it wasn't worth spending one more second of her life wondering about him, and the danger with Vincent's character is that people would give up on him in the book if there wasn't any outcome.

Clare said that we should know more about the alcoholic's family and whether they had tried to help him with Tough Love, or one of those ways of coping.

They hardly dared to look at Gerry since they all knew

it had been the boy's mother who was the alcoholic. Surely he couldn't have a murderous solution to this problem. It was too hurtful, too near home. But you could never tell at a writers' class.

Gerry said that maybe the alcoholic could have killed himself.

'But why would he do that?' Clare asked.

'Out of guilt – maybe he thought that he had done too much to the family already and they would be better if he was gone.'

Vincent put out his hand and laid it on his son's arm. 'She didn't do that, Gerry, it was an accident,' he said, his voice very low.

The other three watched the tableau, hardly able to move.

Nancy didn't know where she got the courage to break the silence, but she spoke in a clear voice as if calling them back to their surroundings. 'Right – only Gerry left, what's your story?'

Gerry read out his typed pages about a boy who saved a man's life in a brawl and the man turned out to have magical powers. 'I'll give you two wishes. But you must make them immediately,' the man said. So the boy said he would like for wish one to go far, far away where no one had ever heard of him and where nothing reminded him of anything. And for wish two, he would like his father to meet someone nice and marry them and have a happy home of his own.

At that moment they were all called to pull their chairs round and hear the lecture.

The Tuesdays went on and none of the little group ever missed one meeting. They saw other tables where people had dropped out. They heard that one man had offended every-one by reading out pornography; and they heard that a steaming love affair had begun between two people at the table near the door and the woman in question was going to leave her husband. But they each wrote their ten pages every week and sent them by email to the others on Monday nights so that they could come to the meeting with considered views.

Nancy's story changed. Her heroine came to realise how selfish the monstrous man was. She considered herself lucky to escape and found happiness in floristry, because the others said you should write about what you know. Jane's sad heroine became less sad and ran a B&B to make a home for the young mother and child. Clare's receptionist managed to implicate the senior executive woman in a financial scam. Vincent's alcoholic hero wrote a letter to his wife to explain, with episodes in his past, why he was so frail. He planned to emi-grate but was stopped in time. Gerry said he hoped that they didn't mind but he was going to write a non-fiction book instead. He was going to make his theme Great Unsolved Murders. He really enjoyed them, and thought he could get a publisher interested.

They had lectures from authors, from agents, publishers, theatrical producers, film-makers, short-story experts. They listened and they learned and they rewrote and came to take themselves seriously. By the end of the twenty weeks they had admitted to other people that they were going to a writers' class, rather than keeping it a deep secret and pretending they were going to the cinema on a Tuesday night. They told their friends they were trying to write a book.

They all had a manuscript to show for it when the course ended, and there was a little graduation party with wine to celebrate. Everyone was allowed to bring a guest or two.

Vincent and Gerry asked their neighbours, who had been kind and supportive in the bad times. Jane asked Lilly to come with her – her little daughter Sophie was over a year old now and bright as a button. Nancy and Clare, who had become great pals as the months had gone by, invited two fellows they had met at a speed-dating evening, both of them perfectly nice men who might well be part of the future but who equally well might not.

They had contemplated inviting the monstrous Ed so that he could see how successful Nancy had become, and the appalling series producer in the radio station so that she would hear all the praise for Clare. But they decided that whatever else they had learned in the writers' course, there was some very important lesson about Moving On.

And when the ceremony was over, and they were having their glass of wine, they said that they would miss each other. They could, of course, meet without the structure of the writing class but it wouldn't be quite the same.

Then it turned out that Clare and Nancy were going to share a big sunny apartment they had found, so maybe they could have the meetings there.

And further it turned out that Vincent and Gerry were going to sell the house where they had so many unhappy memories and move in with Jane. They would help with the B&B guests, take the wordless man for a silent pint now and then, and be there for Lilly and little Sophie. So that was another place they could go for their meetings.

So, they had written their books and that was a huge achievement – but they would still need support. There was all this business of submitting them and coping with rejection and submitting them again. People often fell at that fence.

They would need each other more than ever, the people whose lives had been changed already so much by the writing class …

Contributors' Biographies

Maeve Binchy was born in County Dublin and was educated at the Holy Child convent in Killiney and at University College, Dublin. After a spell as a teacher in various girls' schools, she joined the *Irish Times*, for which she still writes occasional columns. Her first novel, *Light a Penny Candle*, was published in 1982, and since then she has written more than a dozen novels and short story collections, each one of them bestsellers. Several have been adapted for cinema and television, most notably *Circle of Friends* and *Tara Road*. Maeve Binchy was awarded the Lifetime Achievement award at the British Book Awards in 1999. She is married to the writer and broadcaster Gordon Snell.

Ivy Bannister's stories and plays have been published and performed widely in Ireland, England, America and Germany. For her stories, she has won the Francis MacManus award, the Hennessy award and various other fiction prizes. Around thirty stories have been broadcast by RTE and the BBC, and her story 'What Big Teeth' was recently made into a short film in the United States. A collection of her stories, *Magician*, has been published in Ireland.

Norah Casey is Chief Executive of Harmonia. A Dublin-based company, it is the largest consumer and contract publishing house in Ireland, publishing a range of consumer titles including *Irish Tatler, Woman's Way, U, Food & Wine, Auto Ireland, Auto*

Woman, Your New Baby and many contract publications including CARA for Aer Lingus.

Marian Keyes is the internationally bestselling author of nine novels including *Watermelon, Rachel's Holiday, The Last Chance Saloon, Sushi for Beginners* and *Anybody Out There?* Her latest novel, *This Charming Man*, is published in May 2008. Her books have touched readers around the world, and they are published in thirty-five different languages. Over twelve million copies of her books have been sold worldwide.

Alison Walsh is one of Ireland's foremost editors. In 2001 she launched Tivoli, the new fiction imprint from Gill & Macmillan, where she worked until 2005. She has now left to spend more time with her children, continuing to edit on a freelance basis.

Seamus Hosey is a Senior Producer in the Arts and Features Department of RTE Radio. He has presented and produced a wide variety of radio programmes including *The Arts Show*, the book programme *Off the Shelf* and several series of poetry programmes including *The Darkness Echoing, Painted from Memory* and *The Book On One*. He is the organiser of the annual Francis MacManus Radio Short Story competition, and his series *Speaking Volumes* is published by Blackwater Press.

Paula Campbell is a publisher with Poolbeg, one of Ireland's leading book publishers. Poolbeg publishes bestselling novels in the fiction, children's, romantic fiction, non-fiction and literary fiction genres.

Jim Culleton is Artistic Director of Fishamble: The New Play Company and is responsible for the company's distinctive and riveting vision. Fishamble has presented multi award-winning new work in Dublin, nationally and to audiences in the UK, USA, France, Germany and the Czech Republic.

Julie Parsons is an internationally published author. Her novels are *Mary, Mary* (Macmillan, 1998), *The Courtship Gift* (Simon & Schuster Books, 2000), and *Eager to Please* (Macmillan, 2001). A former producer with RTE radio and television, she lives in Dublin.

Gerald Dawe is the author of six collections of poetry, including *The Morning Train* (1999) and *Lake Geneva* (2003). He lectures in English at the University of Dublin, Trinity College, where he is Director of the Oscar Wilde Centre for Irish Writing and Director of the graduate creative writing programme. His first collection of poems, *Sheltering Places* (Blackstaff), was published in 1978. His second collection, *The Lundys Letter* (1985) published by The Gallery Press, was awarded the Macaulay Fellowship in Literature. Other awards include an Arts Council Bursary for Poetry, the Hawthornden International Writers' Fellowship and the Ledig-Rowholt International Writers' Award. In 2007 he published a volume of collected criticism, *The Proper Word*, and a memoir, *My Mother-City*.

Ferdia McAnna is a well-known published author. His novels are *The Last of the High Kings* (Viking, 1991), *The Ship Inspector* (Viking, 1995) and *Cartoon City* (Headline, 2000). The film of *The Last of the High Kings* was released in 1996. He has edited *The Penguin Book of Comic Irish Writing* (Penguin, 1996), and has published a memoir, *Bald Head, A Cancer Story* (Dublin, Raven Arts Press, Letters from the New Island series, 1988).

Afterword

A Final Word of Thanks from the National College of Ireland

We are hugely appreciative of the time, effort and expertise devoted by the contributors to this book. This breakthrough project was envisaged by my predecessor, Professor Joyce O'Connor, through the friendship established with Maeve Binchy. While the publication of the book has taken place in 2008, in reality this is a windfall from the enormous amount of work invested during an earlier era. For some time now Maeve Binchy has been a staunch supporter of the National College of Ireland. She has been hugely generous with her personal time and resources, based on a fundamental commitment to supporting what we are trying to do. Those who know Maeve will also acknowledge her gift as an inspiring coach (and she's not bad fun either!).

It would be remiss not to thank each of the key contributors both to the course and to this book for their expertise and time given so selflessly (Ivy Bannister, Pat Boran, Paula Campbell, Norah Casey, Marita Conlon-McKenna, Jim Culleton, Gerald Dawe, Seamus Hosey, Marian Keyes, Ferdia McAnna, Mary Morrisy, Julie Parsons, Deirdre Purcell, Peter Sheridan, Alison Walsh, Jonathan Williams, Peter Woods and Willie Rocke). Each of the above has their fingerprints on this innovative project and, incredibly, everyone involved waived their entire fees in order to bring this idea to life. Hopefully we've managed to capture the essence of their input with some degree of rigour. Sarah Eustace (former assistant to Joyce O'Connor) was the Project Manager at the college. Once the journal was pulled into manuscript form all the 'technical stuff' (structural editing, copy-editing, negotiating and the royalty fees) was handled with ease and some style by Maeve's long-time agent Christine Green. The complex publication process was simplified under the expert guidance of Juliet Ewers. To each of the above, a sincere thank you.

Within the National College of Ireland our role now is to put your money to good use, ensuring we get a result, as it were. The proceeds from your efforts will be used to encourage people to participate in tertiary education who might not otherwise have done so. And when they do come here, we will do everything in our power to help them become the very best that they can be.

The National College of Ireland currently receives exchequer funding which covers approximately thirty per cent of our total costs. The remaining seventy per cent is made up from part-time student fees, international fee-paying students, a range of commercial activities and philanthropic donations. It is a constantly challenging task to balance the books, and it would not be possible without the enormous generosity of our supporters.

The National College of Ireland is a not-for-profit, third-level educational institution which was founded by the Jesuit Order in 1951. It was established as the 'Workers' College' with the explicit purpose of training employees and managers, side by side, in an effort to promote mutual understanding and reduce the high levels of industrial conflict which were endemic at that time. As the world of work changed, the college expanded from this early industrial relations base.

The 'Celtic Tiger' has brought many benefits to Ireland. In the 1960s only ten per cent of school leavers attended tertiary education, but by 2000 more than sixty per cent did so. Yet, while the opportunity to go to college can be life-changing, it is not embraced equally across all sectors of the community. In some affluent Dublin suburbs, over ninety per cent of school leavers go to college; in other, less advantaged areas, the participation rate declines to less than twenty per cent. The National College of Ireland is fundamentally committed to widening participation in tertiary education. There are many roads by which to climb the education mountain: our job is to signpost each of these clearly and to encourage the climbers. Once we get our students signed up, we then need to ensure that as far as is practical, each person is successful in their studies. To assist us we have a number of support mechanisms in place which are on a par with, or better than, anything in the tertiary sector in Ireland. The student commits to learn; our commitment is to do everything possible to help them succeed.

Together, we make a difference.

Dr Paul Mooney
President, National College of Ireland

Suggested Further Reading

The Cambridge Introduction to Creative Writing by David Morley, Cambridge University Press, 2007

The Complete Idiot's Guide to Writing a Novel by Tom Monteleone, Alpha Books, 2004

The Creative Writing Coursebook: Forty Authors Share Advice and Exercises for Fiction and Poetry by Julia Bell (ed.), Pan Books, 2001

The Creative Writing Handbook by John Singleton, Mary Luckhurst, (eds), Palgrave Macmillan, 1999

Creative Writing: A Practical Guide by Julia Casterton, Palgrave Macmillan, 2005

From Pitch to Publication by Carole Blake, Pan Books, 1999

The Handbook of Creative Writing by Steven Earnshaw, Edinburgh University Press, 2007

How to Be a Brilliant Writer by Jenny Alexander, A&C Black, 2005

How to Write Damn Good Fiction: Advanced Techniques for Dramatic Storytelling by James N. Frey, Pan Books, 2002

How to Write a Novel by John Braine, Methuen, 1974

On Writing by Stephen King, New English Library, 2001

Reading Like a Writer: A Guide for People who Love Books and for Those Who Want to Write Them by Francine Prose, Harper Perennial, 2007

The Road to Somewhere: A Creative Writing Companion by Robert Graham, Helen Newall, Heather Leach, Julie Armstrong and John Singleton, Palgrave Macmillan, 2004

The Routledge Creative Writing Coursebook by Paul Mills, Routledge, 2005

Teach Yourself Creative Writing by Dianne Doubtfire and Ian Burton, Teach Yourself Books, 2003

This Year You Write Your Novel by Walter Mosley, Little, Brown, 2007

Writing a Novel by Nigel Watts, Teach Yourself Books, 2006

The Writing Experiment: Strategies for Innovative Creative Writing by Hazel Smith, Allen & Unwin, 2005

Writing Fiction: A Guide to Narrative Craft by Janet Burroway and Elizabeth Stuckey-French, Longman, 2006

Writing Fiction: Creative and Critical Approaches by Amanda Boulter, Palgrave Macmillan, 2007

Writing Logically, Thinking Critically by Sheila Cooper and Rosemary Patton, Longman, 2006

A selection of writing competitions, awards, etc.

FULL-LENGTH PROSE

Chapter One Promotions Novel Competition
Held once every four years.
For previously unpublished work. The winner will be
supported in completing their novel which will be published
and available through the Book Cellar and Amazon.
*http://www.chapteronepromotions.com/competitions/novel-
competition.htm*

Cinnamon Press Novel Writing Award
The aim of this award is to encourage new authors, enabling
debut novelists to achieve a first publication. The winning
author has their first novel published by Cinnamon Press.
http://www.cinnamonpress.com/competitions.htm

Crime Writers' Association Debut Dagger
Annual crime writing competition. Open to anyone who has
not yet had a novel published commercially.
http://www.thecwa.co.uk/daggers

Harry Bowling Prize
Held once every two years. Open to anyone who has not had
an adult novel published in any genre, including under a
pseudonym. Each entry must be set in London but may be in
any genre and set in any period.
http://www.harrybowlingprize.net/

Undiscovered Authors National Writing Competition
http://www.undiscoveredauthors.co.uk

Write a Story For Children Competition
The Academy of Children's Writers annual competition, open
to all amateur writers over the age of eighteen.
http://www.childrens-writers.co.uk/competition

SHORT STORIES

BBC National Short Story Award
The largest award in the world for a single short story.
http://www.theshortstory.org.uk/nssp/

Bridport Prize
Annual international creative writing competition for poetry
and short stories.
http://www.bridportprize.org.uk/

Fish Publishing Writing Contests
A variety of competitions that change annually from this Irish
publisher. For previously unpublished work only. Winners will
be published in an anthology.
http://www.fishpublishing.com/writing-contests.php

National Galleries of Scotland
Write a poem or short piece of prose inspired by one of the
works in the collections of the National Galleries of Scotland.
The work may be selected from any of the NGS galleries.
Pieces should not be significantly over 1,000 words.
http://www.nationalgalleries.org/education/competition/6:3740/4474/

The New Writer
Annual international prose and poetry competition.
Contemporary work in any genre.
http://www.thenewwriter.com/prizes.htm

New Writing Ventures
Annual award for fiction, non-fiction and poetry. For UK
residents only.
http://www.newwritingpartnership.org.uk/

SCREEN AND STAGE

The Brian Way Award
This annual prize is for playwrights who write for young
people of at least forty-five minutes long. Submitted plays
must have been produced professionally within the past year.
http://www.theatre-centre.co.uk/brian_way_life.asp

The British Short Screenplay Competition
International competition for a screenplay of any genre,
between five and fifteen minutes long, previously not sold,
optioned or produced.
http://www.kaosfilms.co.uk/

The Meyer Whitworth Award
This annual award is to help further the careers of UK
playwrights who have had their work professionally produced
but are not yet well established.
http://www.playwrightsstudio.co.uk/Meyer-Whitworth.html

Stellar Network Open Page
A chance to test your work with an informal industry group at
the British Film Institute in London. Submit your work to an
Open Page evening and get your latest script up on its feet with
the help of attending actors. Must be no more than fifteen
minutes, and can be written for theatre, radio, TV or film. This
is not a showcase but a testing ground. Actively seek
submissions in early draft stages rather than polished pieces of
work. Check the Events List on the website for more details.
http://www.stellarnetwork.com/uk/

USEFUL LINKS

http://www.bbc.co.uk/writersroom/
http://www.channel4.com/4talent/national/
http://www.bbc.co.uk/northernireland/learning/getwritingni/
http://scriptonline.net/home_news.html

RADIO

BBC Radio 4

Radio 4 commissions programmes twice a year.
http://www.bbc.co.uk/radio4/arts/commissioning.shtml
http://www.bbc.co.uk/radio4/arts/commissioning_briefs.shtml

The BBC Writersroom accepts script submissions all year round. Visit the website for rules and submission guidelines.
http://www.bbc.co.uk/writersroom/writing/submission_guidelines.shtml

MAGAZINES

Aesthetica

British arts and culture magazine.
http://www.aestheticamagazine.com/

Ambit

Quarterly magazine that publishes original poetry, short fiction, art and reviews.
http://www.ambitmagazine.co.uk/

Bella

Women's magazine.
http://www.bella-magazine.com

Brand
Literary magazine featuring stories, plays, poems and creative non-fiction.
http://www.brandliterarymagazine.co.uk/

Chapman
One of Scotland's leading independent literary print magazines.
http://www.chapman-pub.co.uk/home.php

Countryside Tales
Quarterly magazine about the countryside.
http://www.parkpublications.co.uk/countrytales.htm

Edinburgh Review
Scottish journal featuring short fiction, poetry and reviews aimed at an educated reading public with an interest in critical thought.
http://www.englit.ed.ac.uk/edinburghreview/index.html

Farthing Magazine
Quarterly magazine featuring science-fiction, fantasy and horror fiction.
http://www.farthingmagazine.com/

Good Housekeeping
Women's magazine.
http://www.goodhousekeeping.co.uk/

Granta
Literary magazine.
http://www.granta.com/

London Magazine
A review of literature and the arts.
http://www.thelondonmagazine.net/

Mslexia
Quarterly magazine for women who write.
http://www.mslexia.co.uk/

My Weekly
Women's magazine.
http://www.jbwb.co.uk/weekly.html

New Welsh Review
Quarterly magazine focusing on Welsh writing in English.
http://www.newwelshreview.com/

People's Friend
Classic magazine containing stories, serials and features.
http://www.jbwb.co.uk/pfguidelines.htm

Random Acts of Writing
Magazine dedicated to short stories.
http://www.randomactsofwriting.co.uk/

Scots Magazine
Scottish interest title.
http://www.scotsmagazine.com/

Scribble Quarterly
The short story magazine.
http://www.parkpublications.co.uk/scribble.htm

Take a Break
Women's magazine.
http://www.takeabreak.co.uk/

The Lady
England's oldest weekly magazine for women.
http://www.lady.co.uk/

The New Writer
Magazine showcasing original writing.
http://www.thenewwriter.com/

Transmission
Independent literary voice for Manchester.
http://transmissionhq.org/

WI Life
WI members magazine.
http://www.womens-institute.co.uk/

Writer Magazine
Resources for writers.
http://www.writermag.com/wrt/

Writers' Forum
Resources for writers.
http://www.writers-forum.com/

Young Writer
Quarterly magazine for children and young people.
http://www.youngwriter.org/